THE
RETAIL
STORE

THE RETAIL STORE

DESIGN AND
CONSTRUCTION

William R. Green

 VAN NOSTRAND REINHOLD COMPANY
NEW YORK

Library of Congress Catalog Card Number 85-31574

ISBN 0-442-22733-7

To Marvin J. Richman

Printed in the United States of America

Designed by Anna Bostroem Kurz

Van Nostrand Reinhold Company Inc.
115 Fifth Avenue
New York, New York 10003

Van Nostrand Reinhold Company Limited
Molly Millars Lane
Wokingham, Berkshire RG11 2PY, England

Van Nostrand Reinhold
480 La Trobe Street
Melbourne, Victoria 3000, Australia

Macmillan of Canada
Division of Canada Publishing Corporation
164 Commander Boulevard
Agincourt, Ontario M1S 3C7, Canada

16 15 14 13 12 11 10 9 8 7 6 5 4 3 2 1

Library of Congress Cataloging-in-Publication Data

Green, William R., 1945–
  The retail store.

  Bibliography: p.
  Includes index.
  1. Stores, Retail—Planning.   2. Stores, Retail—
Design and construction.   3. Shopping malls—Planning.
I. Title.
HF5429.G6794   1986   725'.21   85-31574
ISBN 0-442-22733-7

CONTENTS

PREFACE

The process of conceiving, designing, building, and merchandising a retail store results in some of the most exciting, original, and dynamic of environments. The retail store is the jazzman, the hawker, the pitchman, the titillator— the essence of a capitalist, materialistic society. It is satiating, entertaining, and subservient to the physical, social, and psychological needs of the shopping public. It is expected to be pretentious, frivolous, and fun. The retail store is not considered by experts to be serious architecture and rarely receives notice from those who study buildings for a living. It is a building form as old as civilized man, yet it must always reflect current tastes, fashions, and trends. Stores, unlike most building designs, cannot be too far out of fashion.

The retail store has one of the shortest lives of any type of construction. Store turnover is intense: if one lasts for more than ten years, it is considered unusual. Stores are like flowers that bloom rapidly and die as quickly. Like flowers, however, the beauty, excitement, and value of stores are not diminished by their transience. This aspect only increases the intensity of their expression. The process of designing, building, and merchandising retail stores is part of a continuing cycle of birth and death, leasing and abandonment, construction and destruction. It is the nature of the people who compose the shopping-center industry to search constantly for different, better, faster, and more exciting ways to merchandise, display, and sell products. The people involved must be prepared to take on this challenge. They must be quick decision makers, responsive to change, and skilled in the ways of their professions.

The Retail Store: Design and Construction is intended as a guide to the process of retail-store design and construction for all parties involved: the merchant, the landlord, the designer, and the builder. In this book, greater emphasis is placed on retail stores in shopping malls than on freestanding or in-line, street-location stores. The shopping trends of the past thirty years have made shopping malls the location of choice for stores throughout the country. Indeed, the shopping mall is an entire new industry, one with its own rules, organization, and culture. This book is a reflection of the processes, materials, and

techniques of this industry and is an attempt to detail only the basic requirements and elements of retail-store design and construction.

Each new store is like an original work of art. It is the result of the degree
to which all parties involved in developing the store understand the elements
and requirements of construction and design. To the extent that they are successful in understanding and manipulating these factors creatively, they will
be the developers of successful, long-lived, exciting, and useful retail stores.

ACKNOWLEDGMENTS

I wish first to express my appreciation to those who provided information for this book: the manufacturers who graciously submitted product photographs; the designers who shared their experience and illustrative work; and the owners of the stores depicted.

I also wish to thank the people who assisted directly in the creation of the book: Kenneth Lee, Elizabeth Lewis, and Luis Salomon, for graphics; John Padour, for many of the explanatory photographs; and Kathleen Lawrence, for her incredible word-processing skill and stamina.

Last, I wish to thank my editors, Wendy Lochner and Marie Finamore; my colleague, Paul Knight; my partners, John D. Hiltscher and Donald Shapiro; and my wife, Patricia, for their encouragement, guidance, and direction.

ONE

THE DESIGN AND CONSTRUCTION PROCESSES

Designing and constructing a retail store involves many people: the developer of the shopping center or owner of the building, the leasing agent, the merchant tenant, the designer, the mall or building manager, building department personnel, bankers, builders, tradesmen, store personnel, and (indirectly) shoppers. Typically, a store space will be located and leased, a designer commissioned, drawings prepared and bid to contractors, all within a four- to six-month period (fig. 1-1). Next, the building components of the store will arrive from all parts of the world over a period of weeks. Most will be custom components, designed and fabricated especially for the store, and they will often be complicated and expensive. The components are then assembled in the raw or undeveloped existing space, which at first glance usually shows no promise of the completed design expression. During this period, more construction dollars per square foot will be spent on the retail store than are spent on almost any other building type.

The success of a store depends on the combined efforts of all participants to achieve an appropriate blend of product pricing, quality, and variety; to select the best store location; to provide fine service; to display and merchandise the product distinctively; and to create and construct a well-conceived store design within a set construction budget and timetable. While many successful stores may not excel in all of these categories, their success is usually related to the extent to which the majority of the criteria are satisfied.

The store designer (who may be an interior designer or, most commonly, an architect) typically has no control over the products for sale or the quality of service, but may have an impact on merchandising and the location of the store, depending on the receptivity of the client and the strength of the de-

1

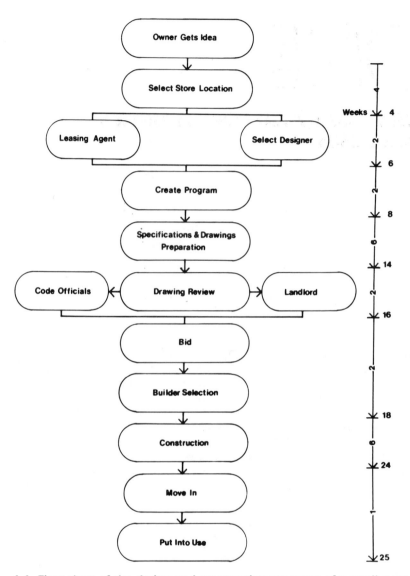

1-1. Flow chart of the design and construction processes of a retail store.

signer's ideas. The designer should, however, have the major responsibility for store design. The designer is responsible for understanding the needs and ideas of a retailer and translating these into a realistic design.

ESTABLISHING STORE LOCATION

The store owner, retailer, merchant, or *tenant,* as he or she is often called, usually begins by deciding that a new store is required. The store may be a new venture, a branch store, or part of a program of store development in many locations. The tenant will research to find the geographic location that offers the best market for the product and then selects a specific location for the store. While selecting a location and negotiating the lease with the landlord, the tenant also chooses a designer. Most shopping centers and buildings require that an architect be commissioned to prepare the store plans. If the store or interior designer is not an architect, he or she may also be commissioned to work with the architect and tenant.

Although the tenant will usually have leased a space before seeking professional design advice, some tenants use the designer's services earlier in the process. The designer can help select a space once the market has been determined, advise the merchant of potential construction costs, and estimate how well the space will satisfy the tenant's program requirements. An experienced designer can spot problems in the physical quality of the space that the tenant may not be able to see. The designer may also review the portions of the proposed lease regarding design and construction, to apprise the tenant of unusual or special building costs or conditions that may be encountered. Last, the designer can help set a realistic date of rent commencement, based on a reasonable construction schedule—rent usually commences sometime after the lease is signed, and the intention is usually to have rent begin when the store officially opens.

SELECTING A DESIGNER

In searching for the best designer, the tenant will probably interview several firms before making a decision. The designer will give the tenant a statement of proposed services and related fees based on the size of the store, projected construction cost, extent of services required, and the time allocated to perform the design services. Services that the tenant will typically ask the designer to perform include design drawings; working drawings; renderings; and assisting in bidding, securing the building permit, monitoring construction, and so on. The fee can be stated within several different structures: as a percentage of total construction cost, ranging from about 7 to 15 percent for full services, depending on the size and complexity of the job; as a flat fee of a given dollar amount; or as a statement of hourly rates, with an estimate of total time to be expended. The latter approach is not recommended, as it is rife with opportunities for misunderstanding and conflict. It is desirable to find a designer who can place all the required design talent under one contract—namely, the designer, architect, engineers, and other consultants. Having the designer take charge of coordinating and supervising the design process will permit the tenant to issue direction through one party, which saves time and minimizes confusion.

The selection of a designer should never be based solely on the design fee, for although this may be an important factor, other factors are equally important. The designer and the tenant must be compatible. While the best designers are flexible and can work well with most any client, some are not able to do so. The design and construction of a store requires the cooperative effort of all involved and the compatibility of these two key players is critical. Tenant and designer should have a preliminary meeting to express their expectations clearly in terms of design philosophy, work procedures, construction cost, and schedule. Also, the tenant should be confident that the designer will have a favorable relationship with the landlord, building department, construction personnel, and tradesmen. Maintaining favorable, nonantagonistic relationships is necessary to get a difficult job done on time and on budget. Finally, the designer must understand and agree with the basic premises of the tenant's retailing concept. A wholehearted agreement on concept will strengthen their relationship and the final product.

PROGRAMMING

The tenant should be very interested in the project design and should be aware of the importance of his involvement in the design process. The best designs are not the sole product of a designer's imagination, but rather are a creative interpretation of the program requirements of a client who knows his product and product market. The designer and the client must both be motivated if they are to achieve a successful design that meets the requirements established by the client and refined by the designer.

At the first meeting with the tenant, the designer should request a detailed program indicating the tenant's functional requirements as well as his perception of the store image, ambiance, and materials. The designer should also request a construction budget from the tenant. It is best if the tenant establishes program requirements on his own, without the designer's assistance. In this fashion, although the program and budget may be incomplete or untenable, the tenant will have been forced to review his thoughts completely as to what is to be built and how much he is able to spend. The designer could assist the tenant by preparing a checklist of possible program items for the tenant's use (see appendix).

When the tenant and designer next meet, they can review the program and budget developed by the tenant. They should define the image of the store: will it be traditional or avant-garde; expensive or inexpensive; emphasize price or high quality; be fun or serious; open or exclusive? For example, the store could sell high-quality, unique merchandise, but at reasonable prices. It could be a fun, lively store designed for a youthful market, with an open, casual atmosphere. The more the store concept can be defined, the greater the possibility the physical reality will capture the essence of the concept.

The functional elements of the store must also be defined. The types of merchandise and percentages of total display area allowed for each must be determined. Special display areas or techniques must be noted as well. The merchant must convey the essence of the product to the designer: at this point, it is a good idea for both parties to visit any other stores the merchant may have and to review stores operated by the competition. Seeing tangible examples helps clarify the product qualities and display techniques the tenant desires. Other questions should be addressed. How will sales be transacted? What type of equipment will be needed? Where will service areas, such as wrapping and repair, be located? The number, size, and type of products to be stored must be known, as well as the maximum or peak level of inventory to be stored. Given the high cost of leased space, it is not usually cost-efficient to allot a disproportionate amount of storage space to stockrooms. Instead, it is a good idea to design stockrooms to accommodate a lesser amount of inventory; the remaining stock can be stored in aisles, offices, under counters or tables, or possibly in other storage areas in the shopping center.

Employee conveniences, such as washrooms, kitchens, and lockers, and office space requirements should also be set at this stage. The number of employees must be known and their respective roles established. Each employee's relationship to customers must be defined. Will he or she be an expert, able to provide detailed advice and information on any product, or will the employee simply stock merchandise and handle sales transactions? If the employee is an expert, extra space may be required for his services. A jeweler, for example, may have a separate office to show his wares.

Security methods and shoplifting control must also be explored. Will electronic or optical sensing devices and cameras be necessary? How will employees help maintain store security? All security equipment that will be purchased by the tenant as well as any other equipment or fixtures he may buy must be known so that the space and mechanical/electrical requirements for these can be established.

The tenant should also give the designer the base drawings of the raw space and the construction criteria of the landlord. If base drawings do not exist, the designer will have to measure the space and prepare drawings. The designer will secure copies of local or state building codes and other applicable regulatory documents at this time. The possibilities of the store's future growth and additional space requirements should also be discussed.

It is not too early to discuss materials at this time, although the discussion should be limited to the general qualities of materials desired. Is the tenant looking for the rich and friendly qualities of natural wood, the coldness of granite, the luxury of marble, the crispness of glass, or the slick and machinelike qualities of plastic and metal laminates? The client's answers will guide the designer, but should not dictate limits at this time.

Often, the tenant will have an unrealistic idea of construction costs, which will be reflected in his financial projections. If the tenant submits an unreasonably low construction budget (one that is 10 to 15 percent lower than the comparable costs of similar stores), he should be educated about current construction costs and asked to increase the budget accordingly. It is best to bring these differences to light early, so the tenant can attempt to get more extensive financing before design and construction begin. Without a realistic budget, it is impossible to design properly. The designer can show the tenant records of the costs of previous stores constructed, or secure a record from the landlord of the costs of other similar stores constructed within a mall. With such comparative data, the tenant and designer can reach an agreement on projected construction costs for the new store. Unknowledgeable tenants should also be made aware of hidden costs within a lease, such as barricade construction, temporary utilities, and other work performed by the landlord at tenant's expense.

Another area of frequent misunderstanding on the part of some tenants is the total time required to design and construct a store. Those who are leasing their first store may believe the store can be designed and built in a matter of a few weeks. However, the average time for store design is about six weeks; the time required to bid the construction is about two weeks; construction can take as little as five weeks for a small, uncomplicated store to several months for a large store; at least one week should be allowed for stocking. Therefore, the shortest reasonable time to design and build a small store is about fourteen weeks. Three to four weeks should be added to the schedule, however, to allow time for landlord and building department approvals, material shortages, and other unforeseen delays. This raises the average time required for the design and construction of a small- to medium-size store to about sixteen to eighteen weeks. While design and construction timetables can and have been shorter, it is best to allocate this block of time, if possible.

With the program, budget, and schedule established, the designer and tenant can then proceed to the next stage, drawings and specifications.

DRAWINGS AND SPECIFICATIONS

The first step in translating the tenant's program requirements into three dimensions is the designer's preparation of the preliminary design drawings (fig. 1-2). These drawings are a first attempt to synthesize the program and budget requirements with the existing space, building code, and landlord requirements. The preliminary design drawings will be schematic, conveying only enough information to express the basis of the design clearly. Typically, the designer prepares a floor plan, reflected ceiling plan, storefront elevation, and a store section. The locations of basic functional elements, such as displays, circulation, and work or storage service areas, will be indicated. Basic materials are also selected and shown in the drawings.

The designer prepares the drawings as a tool for discussion. Ideally, the design will represent the concept the tenant has in mind; if not, complete redesign will be necessary. Most likely, however, the drawings will satisfy most of the tenant's requirements but need further refinement. The tenant often incorporates other program requirements not included or foreseen in the program phase. The preliminary design drawings, new program requirements, and the tenant's other suggestions are now incorporated into another more detailed set of drawings, called *design-development drawings.*

Design-development drawings are the next step in the refining process. First, the designer studies individual product display and store fixtures; reviews construction details; selects exact material samples; and determines the basic design of the store's mechanical and electrical systems. Once these elements are established, the designer usually prepares presentation drawings that attempt to define all of the design conditions of the store. He also develops material sample boards and perspective renderings in this phase. Next, the tenant reviews the

---

1-2. *Facing page:* The stages of the design process and the final product. (*Photography: Karant & Associates, Inc.)*

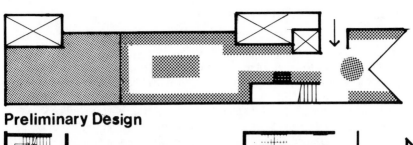

Preliminary Design

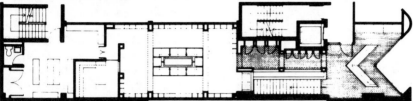

Design Development

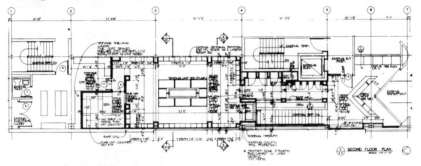

Working Drawing

design-development drawings and, if they are acceptable, forwards them to the landlord for approval. If there are questions about the building code, the tenant and designer may review them with the building department. The designer also prepares a preliminary cost estimate for the tenant's approval at the completion of this phase. If time permits, it is best to wait before proceeding to the next phase. In some cases, the landlord may have requirements concerning such design elements as maximum entrance width, minimum storefront transparency, materials, colors, and the size, type, and placement of external signs. If landlord approval of preliminary design is required by the terms of the lease, the landlord may reject the entire design or some major portion. Although this should not happen if the landlord's requirements were carefully reviewed, anything is possible. The designer should check with the landlord's representative soon after submission, to see if any major problems are apparent. If time is short, the designer may move to the next phase, construction documents, without knowing the exact outcome of the landlord's review.

Construction documents are working drawings and specifications that fully describe the equipment, materials, details, and installation required to construct the store. The drawings are very complete and detailed and include plan sheets, elevations, sections, details, and schedules. Written specifications detailing the methods and procedures of construction can also be provided. In addition, the designer prepares a revised construction estimate for the tenant's approval. Some landlords require the submission of detailed mechanical/electrical calculations and schedule lists. These items and the working drawings and specifications are submitted to the landlord for his review and approval after the tenant has reviewed and approved them. It is very important that the tenant review the construction documents carefully, as this is his last chance to ensure that he is getting the store he desires.

At this time the designer may also submit the construction documents to the building department for review; simultaneously, the documents can be sent out to contractors for bidding.

BIDDING

The purpose of the construction documents is threefold: as the owner's verification of the extent of the construction; to secure bids, which will determine the cost of the project; and to serve as the actual construction plans. The tenant must decide which method of bidding he will use. The first, most common, method is to submit the plans and specifications to three or more general contractors to secure their bids. The general contractor brokers various construction tasks—for example, drywalling, painting, mechanical and electrical jobs—to a group of subcontractors and usually has his own tradesmen, such as carpenters and superintendents, on staff as well. The general contractor may obtain one or more bids from subcontractors in each of the trades. After he and his subcontractors have reviewed the construction documents for about a week to ten days, the general contractor returns a bid reflecting his lowest price to perform the work indicated. If his price is the lowest qualified bid of all the general contractors, the tenant will hire him to perform the work.

The tenant has two other bidding options. He may choose to bid each trade of the job by himself and become the general contractor, or he may choose to become the general contractor but hire a professional construction manager to handle the actual bidding, contract awards, and construction supervision. There are advantages and disadvantages to each method. A general contractor may submit a final bill only upon completion of the job, whereas a construction manager may request biweekly or monthly payments. In the construction-manager system, the tenant makes a series of direct payments to various con-tractors, rather than one lump payment to the general contractor. On the other hand, when a general contractor is used, the tenant may not personally be able to hire or dismiss a subcontractor, whereas a construction manager will offer the tenant a choice of contractors. Both the general contractor and the construction manager offer construction experience that the tenant may not have; both may save him time and money through their expertise. Since tenants are most often busy ordering merchandise and handling other details, they may not have the time or the inclination to become involved in the actual construction. Another advantage of using a construction manager is that he or she can be hired at an early stage, often during the initial design phases. This early involvement permits the construction manager to analyze the pro-posed design methods and materials and suggest alternatives, based on cost and availability. The construction manager can also preorder items that take a long time to fabricate, to ensure their arrival on site on time.

No matter which bidding method is adopted, however, the tenant should select a builder experienced in constructing the type of store the tenant requires. Contractors, construction managers, and trade contractors should be inter-viewed by the tenant to determine whether their interests, goals, and judgments are compatible with those of the owner and designer. The designer should participate in and advise the tenant throughout the interview and selection processes. The builder should be selected not only on the basis of price, but also on the basis of past performance. Is he concerned with the quality of construction, detail, and his ability to satisfy tenant demands? The builder should understand the design intent; suggest realistic alternatives if budget problems are encountered; maintain close supervision over subcontractors; build the job on time and on budget; and work effectively with the tenant, designer, land-lord's personnel, and local building officials.

CONSTRUCTION

The bidding and contract-awarding processes are usually completed within a two-week period, after which construction begins. In reviewing construction, the tenant must remember to channel his comments through the designer or builder, not directly to the tradesmen, unless the tenant is acting as his own superintendent. At first, construction will appear to be progressing very slowly. Materials must be ordered, permits and approvals secured, and demolition work, if any, completed. Then, usually after a week, walls will be laid out and fire protection and plumbing work can begin (fig. 1-3). Next, the ventilation tradesmen complete the installation of ductwork while carpenters build stud

1-3. The first week of construction offers little hint of the final store design.

walls, after which the electricians complete their "rough in." Once the electrical and ventilation systems are in place, the carpenters, drywallers, painters, and other architectural tradesmen go to work. Finally, in what may be the last few days of the construction, carpeting, fixtures, and trimmings are added and the store begins to take on the qualities of the intended design. When the merchandise is taken from the boxes and placed on the shelves and hangers, the retail store looks like what it is: a selling machine (fig. 1-4).

THE MOVE

Depending on the size of the store, the tenant should allow at least a week for this final phase. Merchandise must be unpacked, sorted, stocked, or displayed; the store cleaned thoroughly; employees hired and trained; and all arrangements for utilities made by the tenant. The store lease may require the landlord to approve the construction and the tenant to secure an occupancy permit approving the construction from the building department. Advertisements, announcements, and other publicity must be timed and ordered; bags,

1-4. When construction has been completed, final cleaning and stocking begin.

boxes, wrapping paper, and hundreds of other details must be handled before the store is opened.

Finally, the moment of truth will arrive, and the store will open to the public. Only then will all parties responsible for the store—the tenant, designer, and builder—know if they have succeeded. The total on the cash-register tape will be the clearest indicator of success.

TWO

STORE IMAGE AND SPATIAL ORGANIZATION

The retail store has three major design elements: display areas, service areas, and circulation areas. The relationship or spatial organization of these areas is determined by the same factors that control the layout of any commercial space—the efficient accommodation of the space requirements of equipment, products, and people. In addition, the design of retail stores must satisfy two other factors, which do not affect the design of other commercial installations. Casual passers-by must first be lured into the store and second, induced to buy a product. The sole purpose of a retail store is to sell, and the success of a store is determined mainly by the relationship of sales volume to the total area of the store, or dollar volume per square foot. The extent to which the design of a store plays a factor in increasing total dollar volume is debatable, but the most reasonable view may be to consider good store design a basic element that must exist along with the other important elements of merchandising, advertising, management, product selection, and pricing. The most successful stores are those that consistently maintain quality in all these areas. Therefore, the designer's basic job is to create a functional space that promotes sales.

Designers of retail stores—even the most notable of these—lose sight of these two basic requirements, however. In 1948, Frank Lloyd Wright designed the now famous V. C. Morris store, a conceptual forerunner of the Guggenheim Museum (fig. 2-1). The main display element of the store is a ramp that spirals upward, leading customers past displays of the fine porcelain and glassware. The storefront is a windowless facade of well-articulated brick. Many merchants have occupied the store over the years. Whether the design contributed to the turnover of these businesses is not easy to establish, but the storefront gives

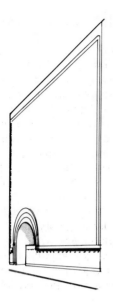

2-1. Rendering of the storefront of Frank Lloyd Wright's V. C. Morris store.

no hint to passers-by that merchandise is available for purchase. There is no sign, only a small display window offering a limited view into the store. The design is certainly a strong expression of exclusivity, but it may have been carried to an extreme: it brings to mind the punchline of an old joke, "The patient died, but the operation was a success."

Successful retail stores live until the cash register stops ringing. The role of the designer is to increase the chances of business success by satisfying all the basics of good store design, by creating a store that is functional, serves the needs of the owner, enhances the product, and captures the interest of the market.

IMAGE

The design of the V. C. Morris store or that of any store makes a statement to the shopping public. When the customer views the store for the first time, he automatically and subconsciously registers an impression of the store's level of service and quality, as well as the approximate price of the merchandise. The visual cues upon which the shopper makes these judgments include the quality of store materials, the type of lighting, the extent of storefront closure, the type of display fixtures, the signs, the pricing techniques, and, of course, the products for sale. Lesser-quality materials indicate lower-priced merchandise, as does unshielded, glare-producing lighting. A well-concealed combination of directional and diffused lighting, on the other hand, indicates an emphasis on the quality of the merchandise rather than low prices. However, a store may sell commonplace, reasonably priced items, yet convey the impression of fine merchandising through its quality lighting and design, revealing the competitive price of the merchandise only through the prominent display of price tags. A closed storefront with small, distinctive show windows displaying a few uncommon, expensive items indicates high-priced goods within; a totally open storefront presents a casual, less threatening image and suggests moderate pricing. Inside the store, display techniques offer further visual cues. If products in the display fixtures appear accessible only with the assistance of a salesperson, the merchandise will seem exclusive and expensive. If products are displayed on flat, open tables, they will appear common and unprotected. Display windows filled with sale signs tell one story; a small, gold-leaf store identification sign on the glass tells another. In short, the way in which merchandise is displayed tells the shopper more about the store than the merchandise alone could reveal. Unless the shopper is an expert in the particular item for sale, merchandise must be evaluated closely, price tags checked, and sales help questioned for the merchandise to tell the whole story. The other visual cues, such as store transparency, signs, lighting, and so on, get the message across before the shopper even enters the store. It is important that external design cues be presented accurately. The overall image of the store must attract the glance of shoppers who will be inclined to purchase the kinds of products for sale and induce them to enter.

Tone is another part of the store's image, and may be playful or serious, active or passive, exciting or subdued. A children's toy store, for example, should be playful in tone, as should an adult "toy store" such as a video equipment store. A rare-book store should have a serious image. A store that is visually stimulating or confusing, with different levels, much written product information displayed, and with all products easily accessible, will best serve a younger clientele. Older customers will expect easy circulation, no change in levels, more service, and a simple, comprehensive presentation of merchandise. If the store design is exciting, visually stimulating, and avant-garde, look for extroverted shoppers to arrive; if the store design is subdued and restrained, prepare for introverted shoppers. Of course, these are generalizations, but a store design is like the front page of a newspaper; some readers will be attracted to the clean, restrained, uncluttered appearance of the *New York Times*, others will prefer a more sensational look. Each is designed to reach a certain segment of the buying population.

A store is a sales tool, like television advertising or the well-worn pitch of a door-to-door salesperson. To be effective, the store must induce shoppers to enter and buy. The psychology of selling is a subject well known to promotional and advertising people and should be of interest to the store designer, since knowledge of this area, applied to store design, can increase sales.

A good salesperson will avoid intimacy with customers. Tom Hopkins (Hopkins 1982, 174) suggests a salesperson should make customers entering a store aware of his or her presence and maintain a friendly but limited initial contact. If the salesperson pushes or crowds the customer, the customer is more likely to flee the store than buy. The customer should want to ask for the salesperson's assistance. Similarly, a store design must not psychologically crowd or intimidate a potential customer. Stored in our genes may be a primal fear of venturing

2-2. The transparent storefront lets shoppers know what to expect upon entering the store. *(Photography: Sadin-Schnair Photography)*

into unknown territory, which may unconsciously be recalled by a shopper as he approaches an unfamiliar store. Therefore, it is essential that the store be designed to permit the shopper to determine easy entry and "escape" routes. The shopper should be able to sense the layout of the entire store, if small, or a significant portion of it, if the store is large (fig. 2-2). This will make the customer feel secure and may entice him to enter. Open, accessible store design can be achieved by providing *transparency*—that is, a good view of the inside of the store through the storefront; by maintaining lower display fixtures in the front of the store, to permit view into the depth of the store; and by not placing a sales clerk behind a counter at the entrance, facing the shopper. This philosophy of design does not automatically preclude the use of a completely closed front, like that of Frank Lloyd Wright's Morris store, but it does necessitate using some sales tool other than the storefront, such as advertising or word of mouth, to induce the shopper to enter.

The designer must create a store that encourages the shopper, once inside the store, to lower his psychological defenses and become interested in the merchandise. If the customer is relaxed and interested, he may then ask a salesperson for assistance, or take the time to evaluate the product himself and subsequently make the purchase. A small- or moderate-size store should have an interesting display of merchandise located immediately adjacent to the store side of the entrance. This merchandise may not be something that the shopper will buy, but the display area will offer him a secure place to browse while he develops an understanding of the remainder of the store. It provides a psychological "toehold." When the shopper feels comfortable, he will move on to other areas of the store. Larger stores should be designed

2-3. Wide, well-marked aisles in larger stores permit shoppers to pass easily from department to department. (Design: Trauth Associates Ltd.; photography: Barry Rustin)

similarly but may be broken up into departments. In designing larger stores, it is important to create a sense of free access to the various departments. Wide and highly visible aisles encourage shoppers who enter to move along to their areas of interest (fig. 2-3).

There are other psychological factors that affect the complex process of shopping, and the development of retail designs for shoppers. In his book *Influence*, Robert Cialdini cites several factors that subconsciously influence people to take action: commitment, social proof, authority, reciprocation, liking, and scarcity (Cialdini 1984, 13). Cialdini theorizes that people use these factors of influence as shortcuts in decision making. Three of these factors—commitment, social proof, and authority—can affect store design and operation, and are discussed below.

Commitment is the desire of humans to be consistent with previous deeds or choices. Once a decision has been reached, people tend to move ahead automatically, convinced they have made the right choice. The store designer should consider this factor of commitment. If the shopper is required to make an effort to enter the store, this commitment to spend at least some time inside may incline the shopper to make a purchase. The greater the effort required, the greater the commitment. Entering a totally open storefront requires little commitment by the shopper: he can step inside, review the store, and leave easily. Passing through a closed front with swinging doors, however, requires the maximum commitment on the shopper's part (fig. 2-4). Of course, any shopper commitment gained by creating a closed storefront may be negated by the number of impulse shoppers who are put off by the barrier. The designer must decide the level of commitment appropriate for the store to be designed. The transition area, which sets the tone of the entrance and resultant degree of commitment, can be more subtle than a swinging door. The designer may use an open, arched passageway or a dropped soffit with a storefront recess. Even subtle transition elements may help to establish a commitment to the store in the shopper's mind.

Commitment may also be established within the store. If a customer can gain access to a product only with a salesperson's assistance, the level of commitment is greater than if the item is on open display, so that it can easily be picked up and evaluated. Also, if the customer must ask a salesperson any questions about the product, the level of commitment to both the product and the salesperson will be higher—chances are greater that the customer will buy the product.

Social proof is a factor of influence rooted in the maxim "if everybody's doing it, it must be okay." Aside from word-of-mouth advertising, a store can convey the message of social proof by attracting people into or in front of the store. Shoppers, viewing many people in a store and not knowing whether they are buying products or only looking, will be influenced to believe the store is attractive (fig. 2-5). To draw customers, the designer should create areas of interest in the store, such as sale merchandise or special displays, and place them so that they can be seen from the street or mall. Establishing social proof may require the designer to create spaces that appear to be filled with people even if they are not. Locating display tables at the front of the store, cramping the circulation somewhat and packing more display than would be dictated

2-4. As she enters through the swinging door, this customer makes a psychological commitment to spend time or money in the store.

by normal functional considerations, will create a busy area, filled with shoppers. If the products in this area are on sale, all the better to draw a crowd. Storefront window displays, if properly designed and merchandised, also draw crowds, which influence other shoppers to enter. Interesting, colorful, even bizarre displays and lighting techniques draw people to the storefront: people are attracted to light, color, and motion.

Authority is another factor that influences people's decisions. People can be influenced to do many things simply because they are directed by an authority figure to do so. Store merchants often rely on this principle to sell their products. High-end items, such as jewelry, artwork, and rare collectibles, are often sold to relatively unknowledgeable customers by the "expert salesperson" method. If the store to be designed relies on such sales techniques, the store design should convey an image of authority. Such symbols of authority as the use of luxurious, quality materials, showcases in which products are accessible only through the authority figure, and traditional product-evaluation areas, which provide face-to-face contact between customer and expert, will enhance the store's apparent authority. Similarly, the display of wall certificates and other credentials and the establishment of a special office for the head expert will fix the authority concept in the mind of the shopper.

A designer's concern for and accommodation of these three factors of in-

2-5. The presence of these shoppers provides social proof that may induce other shoppers to enter the store. *(Design: LUBOTSKY, METTER, WORTHINGTON + LAW, LTD.; photography: Karant & Associates, Inc.)*

fluence may be greeted with disdain by some, who will view them as forms of trickery. While the methods of influence may be misused, their use in store design can be constructive. The shopper's goal should be to buy something he wants at a fair price. The factors of commitment and social proof allow the shopper to feel comfortable with his decision to enter the store: without these, he might never enter the store. Authority can reassure the customer about his purchase. From a store-design standpoint, these factors facilitate the process of decision making and at least help to get customers in the store.

SPATIAL ORGANIZATION

The design of retail stores offers a great deal of freedom from government control. While other architectural types, such as medical and residential buildings, have many building-code stipulations (such as light and air requirements, room size, and ceiling heights), retail stores are relatively unregulated. The main area of regulation with regard to overall design concerns egress. Regulations may stipulate that exit doors swing in the direction of travel, that two points of exit (distant from each other) be provided, that aisles be of a certain width, and so on. Unlike offices or institutions, retail stores are not as controlled by tradition. Wild flights of design fancy are often welcomed by storeowners, landlords, and customers alike. Construction budgets for retail stores may also permit more elaborate design statements than budgets for residential projects. The designer of a retail store may have the opportunity to create design expressions that are both functional and exciting.

The basic space presented to the designer is commonly a rectangle, with the short sides forming the front and rear of the store. Landlords lease storefront space in addition to the total area, and, in both street and shopping-mall locations, usually attempt to strike the proper balance between the width of a storefront and the total store area. Typically, the storefront of a front-to-back store will be not more than one-fourth to one-third of the overall store depth. Thus, a store with a depth of 100 feet will have a storefront width of 25 to 33 feet. Corner stores automatically have more frontage as related to total area, but this is often as much a curse as a blessing, since storefronts are expensive to construct and it is difficult to display successfully to both the outside and inside of the store. Consequently, part of corner-store frontage is often designed to be a blank wall. Certain stores selling products that do not require much space, such as jewelry stores, are well suited to corner locations; others that can successfully merchandise much of their product in large storefront displays, such as shoe stores, are also logical candidates for a corner location. Since rents are always higher for corner spaces, the tenant must consider whether the store will really benefit from the added exposure. If not, an in-line location (a store placed between two other stores in a mall) would be more appropriate.

The relationship of the areas allocated to display, service, and circulation forms the core of the design of a retail store (fig. 2-6). Unlike other building types, retail stores do not usually separate functional areas with walls, except to enclose service and storage areas. Most stores remain as open as possible, to permit the shopper to orient himself easily from any location.

Plan

▓ Display   ▨ Circulation

☐ Storefront Transition   ☐ Service

2-6. The functional areas of a typical store.

Circulation Areas

Circulation paths in small stores are usually defined very simply with front-to-back or loop aisles, while those in larger stores may be more extensive versions of basic grids or loops. Circulation paths should be simple, however. Since the assembled merchandise usually offers a wide variety of visual experiences, creating a complicated circulation route to provide visual stimulation is unnecessary. Also, merchandise is usually displayed in orderly, efficient patterns that dictate simple circulation geometry. Overall, circulation must be simple and clear enough so that the shopper focuses on the displays, not the aisles. If overly concerned about finding his way through the store without bumping into something, the customer will not be able to concentrate on the merchandise and will not find anything to purchase.

The display of merchandise is like a motion picture that requires the viewer, rather than the film, to move. As he passes through the store, the shopper should feel as comfortable as a movie patron sitting in a chair; his focus of attention should be on the product only. If different floor levels are to be used, the designer must be careful to control access between levels with stairs or ramps. These vertical transitions should be easy to recognize. It is unwise to design a continuous single- or double-riser stair across the width of the store. Shoppers often move through a store intently, viewing merchandise; in this frame of mind, they may fall or trip over an unmarked change in elevation. Circulation paths are also the means of emergency store egress, and should be of proper widths to satisfy building-code requirements. The needs of people with physical or visual handicaps should also be met. Designing adequately sized aisle space and adding ramps, rather than steps, will permit those shoppers to become buyers. The visually handicapped will appreciate stores with glare-free lighting and aisles that are clearly defined with special colors or textures.

Service Areas

Service areas can be either work or storage spaces. Examples are cash counters, wrapping counters, offices, storage areas, tailor or repair shops, shipping and receiving areas, washrooms, and kitchens. Service areas are usually designed for maximum efficiency, accessibility, and optimum equipment placement and they are generally located at the back of the store, since areas close to the front are too valuable as selling space to be used for service activities. Also, in many stores, delivery access is at the rear of the store. Moreover, storeowners do not want customers entering private areas; it is therefore best to segregate service areas to the rear of the store.

The location of the cash counter will vary, depending on the size of the store, the number of employees, and whether the store is self-service (fig. 2-7). If the cash counter is located at the front of the store, security controls are increased. However, if the salesperson and cash counter are the first things a customer sees as he enters a store, he may become intimidated. If the cash counter is located at the front, it should be concealed by storefront displays and oriented to face the store interior. However, this arrangement requires a relatively wide storefront and presents security problems when only one salesperson is on duty: if the salesperson is serving a customer at the rear of the

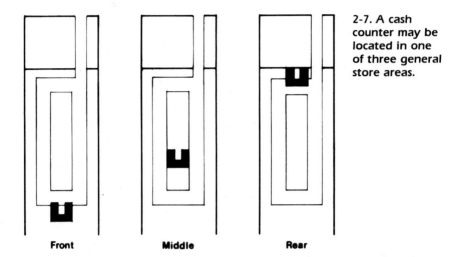

2-7. A cash counter may be located in one of three general store areas.

Front   **Middle**   **Rear**

store, the front cash counter will be unprotected and subject to theft. If the storeowner opts to put the cash counter in the front, at least two clerks should staff the store, with one person stationed at the front at all times.

If the cash counter is placed at the rear of the store, this eliminates the problem of immediate shopper/salesperson eye contact and puts the cash counter in a more secure location. This is the best arrangement for single-salesperson stores. However, the designer must be careful to provide this salesperson with an unobstructed view of the entire store, or security may be compromised. The designer should place high display counters only around the store perimeter, and may choose to install security mirrors or cameras. Finally, the cash counter may be located in the middle of the store. If the store is larger and has many employees, the cashier will probably not need to monitor the store for shoplifters or control access to stockrooms. The centralized location of the cash counter also provides good access for shoppers.

If it can be accommodated, a wrapping counter that is part of, adjacent to, or behind the cash counter is desirable. With the wrapping counter close by, the salesperson need not leave the cash counter unattended to wrap merchandise, which increases security and speeds sales transactions. Sometimes merchandise is displayed on the cash counter to promote impulse sales, but this is a poor design solution for several reasons: displays on low counters may be blocked by customers standing in front of the counter; displays can physically get in the way of cash transactions; and browsers examining the displays can crowd out customers who wish to pay for merchandise. It is usually better to place impulse merchandise near, but not on or in, the cash counter.

Offices for small stores are usually located in a back storage room and limited to a short counter, space for a file cabinet, and some shelves. Larger stores may have space for full-size offices, which are also usually adjacent to storage areas, or located on a mezzanine. Kitchens for retail-store employees are usually spartan, consisting of small counters with space for a coffee machine, a small refrigerator, and possibly a bar sink and a small table and chairs. Although the number and size of washrooms is dependent on local building codes, at least one washroom should be provided as a source of water and to eliminate the need for employees to leave the store. In general, public washrooms are not provided in retail stores, even in stores located far from any public facilities. The problems of security and maintenance of public washrooms usually preclude their installation. Some local building codes require that special-size washrooms be installed for mobility-limited employees. These large washrooms are difficult to accommodate within very small stores, so tenants of very small stores (800 square feet or less) should find out, before preliminary design begins, whether this code applies to them.

Display Areas

Display areas are the heart of a retail store. Display is the mechanism that presents the merchandise to the shopper in its most favorable light and that permits the shopper to evaluate and select products for purchase.

There are two elements to a display: product presentation and product evaluation. The designer must address both functions. The product-evaluation area is usually a space directly in front of the display or adjacent to it where a customer may closely review the product, read any pertinent information related to it, or have a salesperson explain its virtues. Sometimes the evaluation is a two-step process, as in the purchase of clothing. First, the shopper spots a feature display of a product he likes, then selects a particular item of apparel displayed on a rack. Next, while standing in front of the display rack, the shopper removes the item for close evaluation, looking at the product's construction, color, material, and detailing. He may select several similar items as possible purchases and then move to the final stage of product evaluation, which requires him to try on the clothes. In front of a triple mirror, the customer reviews his appearance wearing the product, checking for fit and overall image. After trying on a few other items, he makes a selection and moves to the cash counter. All products being examined for purchase undergo this evaluation process, although some items are simple and require no additional space. For instance, a shopper wishing to buy a daily newspaper need verify only the date, edition, and title of the paper before purchase, and need not remove the paper from the display rack.

If a product-evaluation area is required, it will often take up part of the aisle. The designer should provide sufficient space for shoppers to bypass browsers standing in front of a display and to give those people reviewing products enough space. Behavioral studies have been conducted that indicate people require a zone of space around them to act as a buffer against perceived threats (Eysenck and Eysenck 1983, 249). The amount of space needed varies among different people and cultures, but if the product-evaluation space is not large enough to provide this zone of psychological protection, a shopper may become so annoyed by the constant passage of other shoppers through his zone that he will leave the store without making a purchase.

The spatial relationship between a salesperson and the customer has also been studied (Eysenck and Eysenck 1983, 253). As a salesperson explains the virtues of a product, should he sit or stand face to face with the customer (maintaining a proper buffer zone, of course) or side by side? Psychologically, the face-to-face relationship is a competitive situation, whereas the side-by-side relationship is a cooperative one. Men are often competitive in character and may view strangers who sit opposite them, such as a salesperson, as a threat; women, who may be taught to be more friendly and cooperative, may view a salesperson in a close side-by-side relationship as uncomfortably friendly. Therefore, to establish a male customer's cooperation, the salesperson should approach him from the side. To avoid making women customers uncomfortable, sales help should approach them from the front. If applied, this theory might result in more face-to-face, service-counter displays in a store with women's products than would be designed for a similar men's store.

Robert Cialdini (1984, 25) describes the influence principle of contrast and its effect on the location of merchandise within a store. If a customer is presented with two items, one after the other, his perception of the second item will be influenced by the memory of the first. For instance, if one enters a room with an average lighting intensity after leaving a darkened room, the second room will appear brighter than if it had been entered under different conditions. Salespeople should show customers more expensive products first. This will make other less expensive, but not inexpensive, products seem more affordable. To apply the principle to the display of similar products, the most expensive items should be located in a prominent position in the store and the least expensive elsewhere. The shopper will see the more expensive items first and either purchase them or subsequently see and be pleased with the lower price of the less prominently displayed products. Of course, less expensive does not necessarily mean low-profit. If a customer can be sold an expensive item, such as a men's suit, first, he may also buy lower-priced accessories because he has already psychologically adjusted to the higher price of the first item. This is the major reason that lower-price, impulse items are displayed near cash counters. Impulse items sell easily because they appear relatively low-priced in relation to the overall expenditure the customer will make. Ideally, merchandise should be arranged in a waterfall of decreasing prices. The customer should be able to view accessory products, displayed in order of decreasing price, as he moves from his main, most expensive purchase to the cash counter. Thus, the $300 suit selection leads to the $100 sweater selection, which is followed by the $50 shirt, the $25 tie, and the $5 pair of socks displayed near the cash counter (fig. 2-8).

The retail store stocks three categories of product: staples, convenience items, and impulse items. These will differ for any store. For example, in a men's store, the suits and shirts are staples, whereas ties, belts, and sweaters are often impulse items. Convenience products are frequently common, low-profit items that can be found in most stores; in a men's store, these might be underwear or socks. Most often, staple items are the items wanted by a destination shopper—a person who enters a store with a specific product in mind. Staples should be placed in the more remote sections of the store so that the shopper

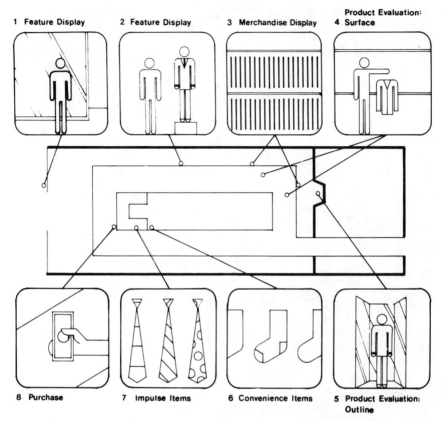

1 Feature Display   2 Feature Display   3 Merchandise Display   Product Evaluation:
4 Surface

8 Purchase   7 Impulse Items   6 Convenience Items   5 Product Evaluation:
Outline

2-8. The ideal customer will follow this sequence of events in the ideal store.

must pass all the merchandise to get to the point of destination. Convenience items may be the intended purchase or may be bought as an accessory to the staple item. These should be located adjacent to the staple items. Impulse or luxury products are not usually a destination purchase. These are sold mainly because the customer has entered the store and been impressed with the displays, product, or price of the impulse item. Impulse items should be located at the storefront and adjacent to the cash counter.

As he passes through the store, the shopper's experience should be varied in terms of the product types, display techniques, and intensity of lighting. The visual experience is sequential, like a movie, and, like a good movie, the store should offer action scenes, thought-provoking scenes, and emotional scenes tied together in a logical sequence. Thus, a storefront may be intensely illuminated with colorful displays; the center of the store may be more businesslike, with displays explaining the quality features of the product or pointing out

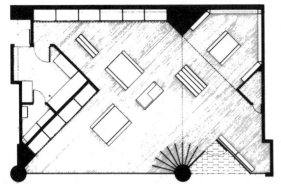

2-9. For maximum visual impact of the colorful merchandise in this fabric store, the entire storefront is made of tempered glass. The basic rectangular space has been changed to a partial cross in plan to make use of the wall surfaces in the display of framed fabrics. The vertical display fixture next to the door pivots 90 degrees for changing displays. Incandescent track lighting illuminates the sales area, and walls are covered in a ribbed, acoustic material that hides damage to the walls underneath when framings are rearranged. *(Architect: Green Hiltscher Shapiro, Ltd.; photography: Karant & Associates, Inc.)*

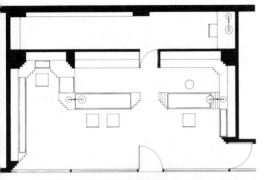

2-10. In this cosmetics store, a horizontal line is continued throughout to provide spatial definition. Intricate detailing is combined with soft incandescent and fluorescent lighting, and crisp, laquered cabinets display the cosmetics. The store had to meet criteria set by various cosmetics manufacturers, such as the requirement for a low counter for product evaluation, which was achieved with the use of steps and setbacks integrated into the overall design. *(Architect: George Gelis & Associates, Inc.; material selections: Arlene Semel & Associates; photography: Jim Norris)*

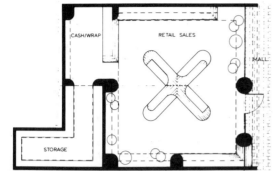

2-11. The design of this small shop is the result of excellent communication between client and architect. The client had a sense of the designer's task—all products had to be displayed prominently, yet be within reach—and was able to provide guidelines without restricting the design. Over 200 styles of men's shoes and related items are displayed, and storage is provided for 1,500 pairs of shoes and boots. The structural column at the entry forms a parti that is repeated throughout the store, providing spatial definition and framing the display and sales areas. *(Architect: Green Hiltscher Shapiro, Ltd.,; photography: Karant & Associates, Inc.)*

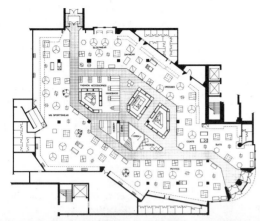

2-12. This is a remodeling of a large (over 20,000 square feet), two-story women's apparel store. A soft, monochromatic color unifies the store and provides a neutral background for the merchandise; a similar-color marble is used on the exterior and repeated in the cosmetics, jewelry, and accessory areas. A well-defined ceramic-tile aisle combined with an angled drop ceiling connects the two entrances and provides easy circulation for the shopper. Much of the existing ceiling and lighting was retained, and incandescent track and spot lighting was added to provide more modern illumination. (Architects: Trauth Associates, Ltd.; store planning and design: HARTMARX Specialty Stores, Inc.; photography: Barry Rustin)

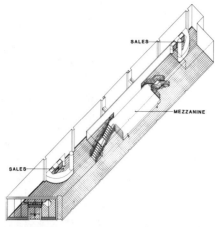

2-13. This medium-size store is located on the second floor of an enclosed mall and is narrow and deep. To minimize the apparent depth of the space, architectural elements were deceptively overscaled; the central stair, for example, uses a thick, 4-inch pipe railing rather than one with a smaller diameter. The neutral, yet distinctive pineboard walls, used throughout, have concealed standards for shelf brackets, and may also be nailed. The entrance, a prominent, trabeated portal in a clear glass wall, suggests classical detailing with its tubular columns and I-beam. (Architect: LUBOTSKY, METTER, WORTHINGTON + LAW, LTD.; photography: Karant & Associates, Inc.)

2-14. This fun and contemporary shop sells cards, notions, and gifts. The store's warehouselike atmosphere is established by the brick walls, diagonal strip hardwood flooring, and continuous overhead truss-track lighting, which also serves as a perch for stuffed animals. The cards are displayed on vertical wall fixtures rather than waterfall-style gondolas, which permits shoppers to get closer to the merchandise. Laminated pedestal cubes are grouped near the store entrance for seasonal displays, and may be removed or rearranged. The store lighting is a combination of incandescent track lights and fluorescent lighting with parabolic diffusers. (Architects: Trauth Associates, Ltd.; photography: Barry Rustin)

the fifteen different types of this product; and further along, displays may be museumlike in quality, evoking a feeling of awe and wonder from the shopper.

Another factor in the design of a store is flexibility of display, which can be divided into two categories: flexibility of store fixtures, and flexibility of fixture layout. Because the retail business is constantly changing, flexibility of design is very important. Styles and product lines go in and out of fashion in rapid-fire sequence. Regular shoppers may become bored with a store that does not alter its displays relatively often to create a new look. To allow the store to adapt to new products and styles and make significant display changes, some flexibility must be inherent in the fixture layout. For example, storefront show windows can be designed to use only movable, temporary display fixtures such as chairs or boxes. Internal display fixtures can be placed on hard-surface floors of wood or tile—heavy fixtures placed on carpeting will leave an imprint. Or fixtures can be designed to use interchangeable parts, so that they can be used for different products and display techniques. Above all, lighting and electrical systems must permit flexibility. Track lighting and floor- or wall-concealed power boxes will allow fixtures to be rearranged freely. Total flexibility may not be necessary or desirable in all stores, but should be considered.

In summary, the designer faces the task of creating a store that has an in-teresting and flexible variety of details, images, and tones, yet maintains a unified, cohesive expression of the products sold, their price and quality, and the level of service. The store layout must direct shoppers along circulation paths that are easy to comprehend and that maximize the exposure of the product in the proper sequence. The following store designs are presented to illustrate some of the many fine design solutions which have been developed to serve the shopping public (figs. 2-9 through 2-14).

THREE

PRODUCT DISPLAY

Product display is a key element of the well-designed retail store. It is also the area of design that demands the most involvement by the storeowner, as he is the one who should know his product and how best to sell it. The store designer must listen carefully to the owner's program requirements and translate them into effective methods of product display. If the product is displayed well, it will virtually sell itself, and it will also convey to the customer the store's image, scope of goods, concept, price range, and intent. Individual products on display are like the individual letters of the alphabet. Alone, they mean little, but when the letters are organized into a pattern and made easily identifiable, they tell a story. As a person scanning a newspaper headline immediately understands the top story of the day, so a customer scanning a store with a well-designed product display immediately senses the store's essence and meaning.

Establishing the correct tone with product displays is important; it acts as an automatic screening device that directs potential customers into the store and turns shoppers with no such interest away. Clarity in display is essential. Good displays are a product of the combined efforts of the store designer, who creates the display areas and fixtures, and the display manager, who organizes and selects the product to be displayed. The store designer's role is to create well-organized displays that maximize the available selling space, which, given the annually increasing cost of leasing, retailers do not have the luxury of wasting. The designer's ingenuity in creating and organizing displays can be a deciding factor in the profitability of a store.

Display fixtures, like other elements of the store, must emphasize the item, not detract from it. The customer should be able to understand the product with a minimum of sales assistance. Providing information about the product at the point of display is an excellent idea. The better the customer can understand the product, the greater the chances that he will purchase it. For this reason, it is desirable to have as much merchandise accessible to the shopper as possible. The customer who can see, touch, hear, taste, or smell a product will become more involved and committed to it. Therefore, displays must be designed from the customer's point of view. The first step in the purchasing process is capturing the customer's interest. This is the primary objective of displays. However, display fixtures also have the cross-purpose of defeating shoplifters. Electronic devices are very successful in reducing theft, but the proper design and location of store fixtures, such as jewelry cases, remains an important factor in this crime prevention.

Store display fixtures should also be designed with flexibility in mind. Flexibility permits new products or sales methods to be introduced and the store's look to be changed periodically. It is important to remember that many of the customers who pass by or through a store do so regularly. Without new displays and other changes to attract them, customers will become bored with the store and shop elsewhere. In freestanding floor displays, this flexibility may be achieved by using fixtures with interchangeable parts, which can be added to, subtracted from, or manipulated into different shapes. Several tube and connector systems that offer this flexibility are available. Pegboard or slot wall systems accept many different support elements, which can form shelves, hang rods, or hooks. In addition, attachments for metal grid ceilings can be placed throughout a store to create a changeable ceiling display system.

The process of developing effective product displays consists of identifying the product's qualities, selecting the display techniques, and incorporating these elements into the final display (fig. 3-1).

PRODUCT QUALITIES

Each product has inherent qualities—size, class, and price—that to a great extent dictate the way it will be displayed. The extremes for these qualities are large and small for size, unique and common for class, and expensive and inexpensive for price.

Size

Large products such as furniture, rugs, and pianos are easy to see and may be displayed some distance away from the customer. They do not necessarily have to be placed in a storefront show window. Large products do, however, require generous space if they are to be displayed properly, as well as enough circulation space around the display to permit the shopper to view it completely. Large products may be grouped or displayed individually, but they must always be thought of in terms of the revenue they generate versus the area they occupy. Large, low-profit objects occupy more space and return less income; using a sample display of large, inexpensive merchandise, for example, would be more sensible than a complete display of all the different item types or a mass display of the same type. Delivered products (the items that the customer

PRODUCT QUALITIES

Size	Class	Price
large	unique	expensive
small	common	inexpensive

DISPLAY TECHNIQUES

Presentation	Product Support	Integration
massed	from above	contextual
individual	from below	isolated

DISPLAY FIXTURE PROPERTIES

Customer Access	Product Support	Fixture Types
accessible	rod	horizontal
inaccessible	shelf	vertical

3-1. The final display of a product depends on the product's qualities, the display techniques chosen, and the properties of the display fixture.

buys, as opposed to the floor samples) would then be stored elsewhere. Large products should form the backdrop for smaller products, since large items are still visible at the perimeter of the display. Extremely large products, such as furniture, appliances, home-improvement tools, and pianos, are difficult to relocate, which could result in stagnant, permanent displays if flexible displays of smaller products are not placed nearby.

Small products, such as jewelry, eyeglasses, and coins, are hard to see and must be brought close to the shopper's eye level to get his attention. Products like jewelry are best displayed close to the front of the store in eye-level cases. Small products may be displayed individually, but require a greater intensity of lighting than do large objects, since there is less surface to reflect light. If greater visual impact is desired, small items can be grouped together to form a large, eye-catching mass. If small products are not massed in display, however, they present a maintenance problem—small items are easier to steal. In addition, if display merchandise can be handled by the shopper, the shopper may replace the product on the display without concern for its position or relation to other objects, making it necessary for store personnel to rearrange the products on display constantly. For these reasons, small, individually displayed products should be available for evaluation only with a salesperson's assistance.

Because they are so easy to relocate, small products allow for flexible merchandising. They return more income per square foot of leased space than large objects do, and so should be placed on display rather than stockpiled in a storage area. Of course, the number of products to be displayed and the type of display fixtures to be used will depend on the size and other features of the product.

Class

From a display standpoint, unique products are those that are either one of a kind, of limited quantity, unusual, or that have attributes generally unknown to the public. These high-class products include jewelry, rare coins, artwork, custom-made goods, unbranded items, unusual items, such as gadgets or special tools, and products that are living or a product of nature—pets, distinctive plants or flowers, sometimes even fruits or vegetables. It is difficult for cost-conscious shoppers to evaluate the price of such special products. Since unique items have special, often subtle, qualities that set them apart from similar products, pricing may be based on these special qualities as well as their inherent value. The price markup on rare or unusual goods can be considerable since the real value is not easy to determine; pricing may be based on such intangible qualities as rarity, beauty, quality, construction, or faddishness. The "sizzle" of unique products like jewelry or artwork sells more often than the "steak." Buyers are sold on the uniqueness of the product.

To sell the "sizzle," unique products usually require more explanation of their attributes, either in written form or from a salesperson. Greater effort is required to display rare and beautiful objects; special lighting or individual display cases may be needed to highlight the qualities of the merchandise. Unique items may be impulse or destination products, but in general, the shopper may be familiar with the store but is probably not aware of the specific items for sale until he reviews them at the store. This is contrary to the purchase of such common items as cigarettes, newspapers, name-brand clothing, or appliances, which are true destination products.

Common products are those that may or may not have special attributes but their attributes are so well known that only limited amounts of display effort or verbal or written information is required to sell them. The differences among similar items produced by several manufacturers are small; at times, the only way to distinguish one common item from another is by its advertising or promotional program, such as generic aspirin versus Bayer. From a store designer's viewpoint, however, both aspirin items are in the common class.

Common products may also include items that would be unique but for extensive shopper awareness of the product. Electronic equipment, home appliances, and other such items often have special qualities that distinguish them from similar products. But because the attributes of such products are well reported by consumer product reviewers, advertised in the media, or made known by word of mouth, their distinctive qualities are assimilated and the products become common commodities. An example of this transition would be the Sony Watchman pocket television. When it was first introduced, it was unique but its qualities became known to the shopping public very rapidly. Eventually the Watchman became so well known that it could be sold simply on the basis of price. No special display or explanation was required to sell the product—what was first unique became a common item.

Common items may be displayed in groups of similar or different items, or they may not be displayed at all. In the latter case, only a sign may be required to notify the shopper that the product is available. Displays of common products are intended first to indicate availability, and second to state the sale price. However, even considering these simple requirements, common products need not be displayed boringly. Though the individual products are commonplace, they may be displayed massed or in sequence to provide visual excitement.

Price

Products range in price from expensive to inexpensive and each extreme requires different display treatment. Expensive and unique items must be carefully displayed to make them look expensive and unique. Products that are inexpensive and common must reflect those qualities when on display. People should be able to judge the relative price of the product by the way it is displayed. If a customer is shopping for price only, he may be turned off, without even seeing the price, by a display that looks expensive. Similarly, a shopper looking for unique items may be misinformed by a display that seems to cheapen the product. Price is a relative factor, based on one product's price as compared to the price of similar products.

Price affects the prominence of a product display. More expensive items probably have a higher markup and should therefore be sold in more extensive and elaborate displays. Less expensive and bargain items can sell themselves in simple displays.

Some unusual approaches regarding the successful pricing of merchandise have been suggested. Robert Cialdini suggests that higher-priced products may attract shoppers to buy more than they would if the same items were discounted (Cialdini 1984, 15). He believes that people, whenever possible, make decisions based on routine patterns of action and that most people may have a patterned, automatic response that dictates the purchase of more expensive items, on the assumption that they provide a higher level of quality. In other words, shoppers may buy a product more rapidly if it is overpriced than if it is discounted. This theory may be valid only with regard to unique products, however. People may be more inclined to buy common products based on the best price because they are aware of all the product's features, or because there is no difference among brands. On the other hand, customers may buy the most expensive wine, a unique product, because of its high price. Consumer knowledge of the product is the key to proper product pricing. Of course, manufacturers of brand-name, heavily advertised, common products have been very successful at persuading shoppers to buy their higher-priced item instead of the cheaper generic items. In effect, these manufacturers attempt to create a unique quality in an otherwise common product by creating a brand. A product may, for instance, become the "Cadillac of paper clips" to justify the difference in price between it and similar, less-expensive paper clips. In this case, those paper clips, although not in the unique display class, should be displayed prominently to distinguish them from lower-priced paper clips.

DISPLAY TECHNIQUES

After the designer evaluates a product to determine its size, class, and price, the proper display techniques of presentation, product support, and integration with related products must be selected.

Presentation

Products may be displayed either in a mass or alone, based on the most significant quality of the product—class. If the product is unique, it should usually be displayed to enhance its individuality. A fine painting, for example, should be distinctively displayed on a wall, with no other paintings displayed above or below it. Similarly, individual attention should be apparent in the display of fine furs, jewelry, pottery, or rare coins.

Common products often benefit from mass presentation, arranged by product color or type or a combination of the two. A shop selling sweaters may group them for display by color rather than size (fig. 3-2). This kind of display creates a strong mass of single colors, which is attractive and also helps the shopper to find a specific color. Massing products by type also provides impact and shopper convenience, as shown in figure 3-3. The advantage of mass display is that it offers more visual impact than could be generated by isolating the individual product. Mass displays are common in food stores; even such common items as toilet paper are massed at aisle ends to a point of significant display impact.

Products that are neither unique nor common can be displayed in mass groups with a single product featured at the front. A mass of colorful teapots

3-2. Clothes can be grouped by color to form a massed display.

3-3. Ties can be grouped by style to form a massed display. *(Photography: Sadin-Schnair Photography)*

may be displayed with one teapot specially illuminated and positioned in front to detail its features to the shopper for evaluation. In this type of display, the individually displayed item functions as a display sample while the mass of products behind is the stock.

A massed display of products that are only generically similar, such as televisions, may be desirable. A spectacular mass-display effect can be achieved by setting all the different sizes, makes, colors, and styles of television sets to the same channel. The resulting effect is similar to a large kinetic sculpture. Expensive items are sometimes presented in mass displays, but most often inexpensive or moderately priced products are presented with this technique. Expensive items are usually isolated in individual displays to enhance the product's uniqueness and justify the higher price to the shopper. Large items, too, are less often massed than are small items, which often require the visual impact of massing.

Product Support

Product displays can be further defined by their method of physical support. Merchandise may be suspended from above or supported from below with, for example, a hook or a shelf, a hanger or a pedestal, the ceiling or the floor. The designer's choice of support method will be based on the object's physical qualities and the kind of display emphasis desired. Large or heavy items, such as furniture or pianos, will be supported from below by the floor. Other items that cannot easily be hung from above, such as bottles, books, and bowling balls, belong on shelves. Tennis rackets, paintings, and dresses all display best when supported from above. Tennis rackets do not stack well and are better hung from hooks; paintings are cheapened by a shelf display, and dresses collapse into a wrinkled lump unless they are displayed from above.

Some items may be displayed either way, depending on their packaging. Men's dress shirts may be displayed hanging, or, if packaged, may be stacked on shelves. A designer shop may have all its items of apparel displayed hanging to accentuate their qualities. A discount clothing store may pile its items of apparel loosely on a table to emphasize that the garments are common and inexpensive.

Frequently, inexpensive items are priced higher because of their special packaging. Such small, common items as buttons, screws, or electronic parts, which would be grouped in a bin if loose, can be hung from hooks if they are specially packaged. The products should be displayed largest face out, to give the shopper easy access. Often, special packaging and hanging displays can magnify the product's price many times. The packaging and handy display make the customer's selection easier and his concern for price will be overshadowed by the aspect of convenience. The trend away from shelf displays in favor of hanging displays of common items has been a significant retailing event over the years and is the result of better packaging methods. Today, almost all impulse items are packaged and hung on display, a better display method than the former practice of grouping small products in a visually indistinguishable mass on a shelf.

Certain products, which physically could be displayed either way, must be displayed in the way they would be typically viewed by shoppers outside the store. Thus, shoes are displayed supported from below and hanging light fixtures, wall clocks, purses, and men's ties, which are typically viewed supported from above, are generally displayed in that fashion.

Integration

The final display technique is product integration. Products may be displayed isolated or in context with related products. For example, a man's tie may be displayed with many other ties but without regard to other related items of men's apparel or it may be displayed on a mannequin with a contextual display of tie, shirt, suit, belt, and hat. Similarly, a vase may be displayed isolated or with flowers; dinner plates and cups may be displayed alone or with utensils, placemats, a tablecloth and table.

The choice of isolated or contextual displays may be based on the impact a contextual display would have. If the product will sell well from an isolated, nonintegrated display, then it should be displayed in that fashion. Contexual displays consume more space and are more expensive (fig. 3-4). Of course, a common bar of soap need not be displayed in a soap dish and a pair of men's socks can usually be displayed isolated. But if the soap is in the form of a carved duck or if the socks are knee-high and tie-dyed, then both products might benefit from a contextual display. Contextual displays help the customer make the purchase. Most people are inadequately trained in visualization and require some contextual integration to assist them in the selection of products offered in a variety of styles or colors. Men's clothing is a typical area for contextual displays. Since men's wear is often purchased by women for men and women cannot try on the product, contextual displays are very important sales tools. This same logic applies to women's lingerie departments, where men do much of the purchasing. If the customer sees a contextual display, such as a room attractively wallpapered for display, he may buy the product. If, on the other hand, he sees an isolated roll of wallpaper, he may remain undecided and not purchase the item. The sales power of contextual displays is immense. Customers prefer to have their decisions made easier. Featured items, such as new or sales items or high-profit items, are frequently displayed contextually.

Jewelry, hats, eyeglass frames, and other products that the customer can try on easily may not require a contextual display. Some products, like cosmetics or perfume, are so personal that they may be "displayed" only on the individual customer (fig. 3-5).

DISPLAY FIXTURE PROPERTIES: ACCESS AND SUPPORT

Display fixtures must be designed or selected to accommodate the product's qualities and chosen after the appropriate display techniques have been determined. Each display fixture has three basic properties: it allows or excludes customer access; it permits the product to be displayed from a rod or a shelf; and it is horizontal or vertical.

Display fixtures either give the shopper access to the product or permit him to view the product but restrict his ability to reach it on his own. Stores, whether

3-4. Contextual displays, such as mannequins, integrate different products.
(Photography: Sadin-Schnair Photography)

self-service or customer-assisted, usually have display fixtures that are both accessible and inaccessible. Several factors influence the designer's selection of display fixtures: product security, danger, fragility, and uniqueness. Security requirements are based on the price of the product in relation to its size. Small and expensive objects are in demand and easy for shoplifters to conceal. Large products are more difficult to steal, and products that are inexpensive are not worth the risk to steal. Not surprisingly, jewelry, coins, cameras, watches, mini-televisions, and radios are usually placed in fixtures that are not accessible to the shopper.

Another reason to limit access to a product is if it is hazardous in nature. If the product could injure someone who grabbed it, its display fixture should prevent access. Guns, knives, saws, and animals should be kept under lock and key. Products that may be damaged by improper handling should be accessible only under a salesperson's supervision. Fragile artwork, crafted glass and pottery, rare coins or books, and even fragile flowers, such as orchids, would fall into this category. Last, a storeowner may decide that certain unique products must be inaccessibly displayed. A display that requires the customer to ask permission to see a product makes the item more exclusive and, therefore, more desirable. Any rare or distinctive product may qualify for this attention. Whole areas or rooms can be created that will be accessible only to escorted customers, such as fur vaults, wine cellars, and special display salons. Restricting customer access is used as often as a sales technique as it is for security purposes.

As discussed earlier, products can be supported from above or below, with rods or shelves. The rod may also be a hook, arm, pin, or clip. The shelf may also be a bin, box, rack, platform, or pedestal. Once the choice of support is made, the best technical solution must be determined in consideration of the other display factors.

3-5. Perfume displays involve both the visual and olfactory senses. The evaluation of the product's scent follows the visual enticement of the display. (Design: Gelis & Associates, Inc.; photography: Jim Norris)

DISPLAY FIXTURE TYPES

Display fixtures can be either horizontal, as an island or counter display, or vertical, placed up against a wall or forming a wall.

Horizontal displays, as shown in figure 3-6, are frequently used for feature displays and impulse items. Since they are low in height and do not obstruct vision across the store, horizontal fixtures can be placed in the center of the store in the highest traffic areas—the best areas for feature and impulse item displays. Horizontal fixtures can be used as sales or wrapping counters, and are ideal for the sale of products that require a salesperson's assistance. The salesperson can explain or demonstrate the product from across the top of the fixture while the customer stands or sits in front. If both large and small products are sold, the larger items are usually displayed in taller fixtures at the perimeter walls, which permits shoppers to view the entire store.

Vertical fixture displays, as shown in figure 3-7, are excellent for products that require a backdrop in the display, such as paintings or products with sculptural qualities. They may also be successfully integrated with continuous overhead soffit lighting. Products such as books, shoes, and boxed items are well displayed vertically. Vertical displays permit a concentrated stacking of modular and nonmodular products displayed from knee height to a point overhead.

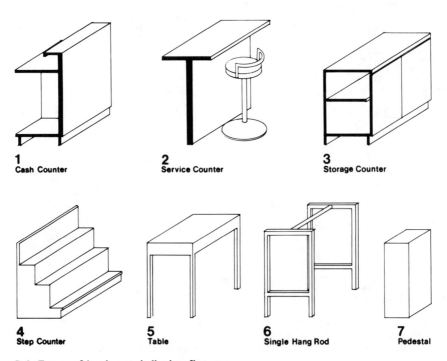

1
Cash Counter

2
Service Counter

3
Storage Counter

4
Step Counter

5
Table

6
Single Hang Rod

7
Pedestal

3-6. Types of horizontal display fixtures.

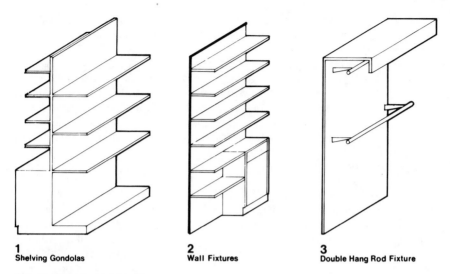

1
Shelving Gondolas

2
Wall Fixtures

3
Double Hang Rod Fixture

3-7. Types of vertical display fixtures.

Horizontal Fixtures

Cash counters are the salesperson's island of refuge, the "business end" of the display floor, the place where a sale is consummated, and often the point of sale for accessories or impulse buys. Typically, the space allocated for cash counters is minimal because space must be devoted to sales first and the counter must function very efficiently. The size of the counter is determined by the equipment, wrapping spaces, and storage it must accommodate, the size of products to be handled, and the maximum number of store personnel who will work behind the counter at one time. Cash-counter equipment includes wrapping equipment (knives, scissors, tape dispensers, staplers, and so on); telephones and intercoms; cash registers; calculators; security monitors, if necessary; and charge-plate machines. Storage must be provided for blank and completed credit-card receipts, bags, boxes, wrapping paper, and office supplies. Adequate counter space for wrapping merchandise must be provided; often, a back counter is used so that wrapping does not slow sales transactions.

Service display counters are used to display products that require a lengthy demonstration or explanation, such as jewelry or cosmetics. The customer is seated in a chair or stool and the countertop functions as a desk. The countertop and front are usually glass and the products inside are not accessible without the help of a salesperson. Light fixtures are often installed within the case to solve an otherwise difficult lighting problem.

Storage display counters are similar to service display counters but are used for briefer sales demonstrations, as no seating is provided for the customer. Instead, the area below the display is used for storage.

Step counters resemble a short flight of stairs and consist of a series of adjacent display platforms, rising one above the other. They are used to display taller products with a backdrop, and provide greater separation and isolation of products than do the flat surfaces of service or storage display counters. Step counters may be glazed to control access or left open.

Tables are unserviced, fully accessible horizontal displays. They are typically used as center islands and often display feature or impulse items. The height of the tabletop depends on the height of the merchandise sold; essentially, customers should not have to bend down to reach the product sold. Small items such as paperback books would be displayed on a table 30 to 36 inches high, whereas larger items, such as bicycles, would be displayed on a lower table, such as an 8- to 12-inch-high platform.

A single hang rod is a low-height horizontal rod suspended at either end by a self-supporting post or panel. Casual clothing such as sportswear is usually displayed on this type of unit. The rod can be mounted at different heights to accommodate items of varying sizes. For example, men's suits are typically hung on a 42-inch rod; slacks on a 54-inch rod; and overcoats on a 63-inch rod. The 54-inch rod is selected most often because it is low enough to see over, but can display several different items of apparel at once. Sometimes the fixture has a series of stepped-down hooks that form a waterfall island display.

Pedestal displays are featured elements used to isolate and highlight specific products (fig. 3-8). A pedestal may be a full-height mannequin or a flat surface supporting a product or a partial mannequin. Pedestals can be constructed at different heights and grouped together to form multiple feature displays.

Vertical Fixtures

Shelving gondolas are vertical shelves used as island displays, and are tall enough to display merchandise clearly without obstructing a view of the entire store. They do not form a wall, but are commonly used back to back. In place of the lower shelves, gondolas may have a storage unit for empty boxes or stock merchandise; the unit may have integral light sources.

Wall fixtures are full-height vertical units that commonly have either shelves or hooks for display, as shown in figure 3-9, or lower storage areas instead of shelves or hooks. Typically, wall fixtures have continuous overhead soffit lights.

Double-hang-rod fixtures are the workhorse displays of clothing stores. They are located on perimeter walls, or, if used as back to back islands, they effectively become perimeter walls. Triple-height racks are sometimes used in price-oriented stores; if so, a catwalk must be provided for access to the top rack. The lighting of double-hang-rod fixtures and the position of the rod must be well designed. The lower rod should be 3 inches forward of the upper rod, and a continuous soffit lighting fixture should be placed about 6 inches in front of the edge of the lower product to illuminate both racks evenly. Adequate illumination must also be provided in front of the racks for product evaluation (fig. 3-10).

DISPLAY FIXTURE MATERIALS

Display fixtures may be constructed of almost any material. Glass, wood, and plastic or metal laminate are commonly used because they are relatively easy

3-8. Playful pedestal displays of stuffed animals combined with wall fixture displays. *(Design: Trauth Associates Ltd.; photography: Barry Rustin)*

to construct into the many different shapes required for display (fig. 3-11). However, almost any other material may be used to construct displays. Marble, granite, cast iron, glass block, concrete block, metal, brick, and tile have all been used with varying degrees of success. Sometimes a designer will want to achieve a contrast between rough display surfaces and the fine surfaces of the product for sale. While such contrast often produces an interesting effect, the designer should be aware of the potential problems. In general, the display surface should not compete with or physically damage the product. Fine watches, for example, could not be displayed on a concrete block surface without risk of breakage. The design of display fixtures offers great freedom of expression, but the designer must present the product properly for shopper interest to be piqued and evaluation to occur. The product and the user must be carefully considered; elaborate fixture designs may yield to practical requirements.

3-9. Wall fixtures can be used to display a gallery of products. *(Photography: Karant & Associates, Inc.)*

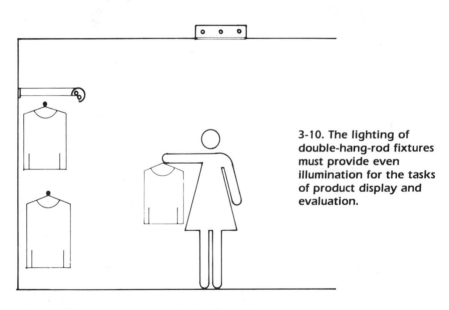

3-10. The lighting of double-hang-rod fixtures must provide even illumination for the tasks of product display and evaluation.

Product Display   Product Evaluation

3-11. Glass, gypsum board, and plastic laminate can be used as product-display surfaces. *(Photography: Karant & Associates, Inc.)*

The designer may have the choice of using either stock or custom-designed and -built store fixtures. Stock fixtures are available for almost every type of casework a store might require, and are usually, but not always, less expensive than custom-built cases. However, when budget permits, using well-designed custom fixtures can be very important to establishing the store's image. Custom fixtures can also provide creative display solutions for small or unusually configured stores. In addition, custom fixtures are easier to integrate with the other design elements of the store—the storefront, walls, and ceiling—to create a unified design.

Very few solid-wood fixtures are used today because of their prohibitive cost. More commonly, wood veneers are laminated to less expensive core materials, such as particleboard or plywood, to create the fixture. Hardwood (oak, walnut, teak, and so on) and laminated-surface display cases are constructed in a similar manner. Cabinet casework is constructed in three classifications of quality, as established by the Architectural Woodwork Institute (AWI): premium, custom, and economy grade. Premium- and custom-grade cabinets make use of higher-quality materials and construction than does economy-grade casework. Custom-grade materials are usually specified for store casework. The designer should review AWI standards (available in the AWI book *Architectural Woodwork;* see the Bibliography) and ensure that AWI specifications are followed by the cabinetmakers who construct the store's casework.

Wood-finished display fixtures are warm, rich, and durable. They cost about the same as plastic laminate finishes, so the decision to use one or the other becomes one of aesthetics and durability. Hardwoods are traditional and may be used successfully to display almost any product that requires a conservative look. If the wood grain competes with the fine detail of some products or a more contemporary look is desired, softwoods or plastic laminates may be used to finish the fixtures.

Softwoods such as pine and fir are used with solid material construction to create fixtures with a more casual appearance. Softwoods can be painted, stained, or finished with clear varnishes. However, softwoods dent easily, are not very durable, and do not permit precise detailing. In addition, softwoods are not dimensionally stable; they grow and shrink under different temperature and humidity conditions.

Plastic and metal laminates are very popular finishes for display cases. In addition to providing a durable, hard, and easy to maintain surface, they are available in many different colors and textures. Laminates may be bent to form curved shapes and are dimensionally precise and stable, two characteristics necessary for high-quality cabinetry.

Glass used in the top or sides of the fixtures displays products while limiting access. Glass can also be used for cabinet doors, shelves, or the structural material of the casework (fig. 3-12).

DISPLAY FIXTURE CONSTRUCTION

Display cabinets with doors can be finished with a variety of detailing techniques. Opaque or transparent materials can be used for swinging or sliding doors, and many different types of hardware are available as well (fig. 3-13).

3-12. Glass is an excellent, unobtrusive medium for displaying glass merchandise.

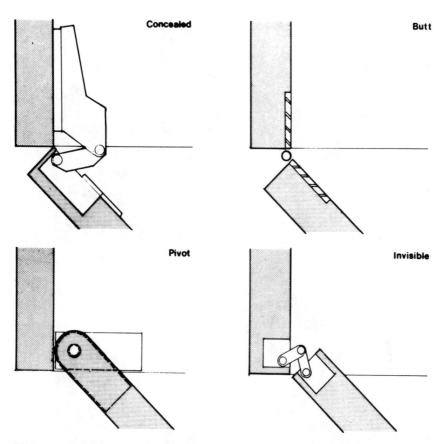

3-13. Four basic types of cabinet hinges are available.

Swinging-door hinges may be either exposed or concealed. Butt, wraparound, or pivot hinges, the traditional types of exposed hinges, are easy to install, strong, and moderately priced, but are, of course, visible when in place. "Invisible" concealed hinges must be mortised into the cabinet and door and thus are difficult to install; European-style concealed hinges, which can be surface-mounted, are easier to install, but are more expensive and not as strong as "invisible" hinges. Nonetheless, European-style hinges are quite popular, because they are concealed, require no catch, and provide a clean, uncluttered look when used with flush overlay cabinet construction. Cabinet pulls are available in a multitude of shapes, sizes, and materials. If a contemporary look is desired, simple wire pulls or their plastic counterparts may be used. For a very clean look, pulls may be eliminated by installing concealed finger recesses at the top or bottom of a door (fig. 3-14).

Sliding-door hardware consists of the tracks in which the doors slide and

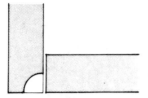

3-14. Recessed finger pulls, shown in section, give cabinetry a clean, unbroken appearance.

3-15. *Right:* A center-pivot glass hinge.

the pulls or rings used to move the doors sideways. Sliding-door tracks may be partially or completely concealed by the cabinet material at the top and bottom, but will be visible when the door is opened. Door tracks may be made of aluminum or plastic and a variety of anodized finished or plastic colors. Sliding-door pulls may be surface mounted or recessed into the door.

Frameless glass doors require hinges and tracks specially designed for that purpose. Glass hinges may be center pivot or offset pivot. In the center-pivot design, a short channel is affixed to the top and bottom of the glass (fig. 3-15). Attached to the channel is a pin that is set into a sleeve embedded into the cabinet; the hinge pivots in this sleeve. This type of hinge requires no drilling through glass and therefore permits easier adjustment. The offset pivot requires a hole to be drilled in the glass (fig. 3-16). Small round plates are set into the glass and attached. The side of the cabinet receives the other half of the hinge and the two are attached, interlocked, and held in place with a pin. Glass sliding doors glide in aluminum tracks on ball bearings for smoother operation. Since the lock mechanism is fully exposed, however, it is difficult to lock the glass doors unless sliding doors with push-button locking are used. For hinged glass doors, conventional cam locks may be installed in the glass, or a solid hinged panel that swings in front of and partially covers the doors may be used to keep the doors closed (fig. 3-17). This solid hinged panel hides the inner parts of the cam lock normally exposed through the glass doors.

Drawers require glide hardware and pulls. Drawer glides are rated according to load capacity, mounting, and extension. Load capacities range from 50 pounds to over 100 pounds per glider, with the standard commercial designation being 75 pounds. Glides may be side, bottom, or top mounted. Side mounting is the standard configuration for drawer glides. Top mounting is used for undercounter drawers, bottom mounting for pull-out shelves. Glides can extend the entire drawer body out of the cabinet (full extension), or extend all but 4 to 6 inches of the body (standard extension). Glides are available that

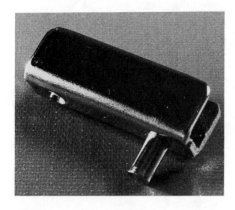

3-16. *Left:* **An offset-pivot glass hinge.**

permit drawers to be self-closing, to lift out, and to prevent unintentional opening. Sliding-drawer pulls are similar to door pulls and may also be eliminated for flush designs by using concealed finger pulls.

The construction of cabinets with swinging doors or drawers falls into four different styles: conventional flush with face frame; conventional flush without face frame; flush overlay; and reveal overlay (fig. 3-18). In conventional flush construction, with or without a face frame, the door and drawer faces are flush with the face of the cabinet, permitting the use of different drawer and door thickness. This style is expensive, however, because of the narrow gap

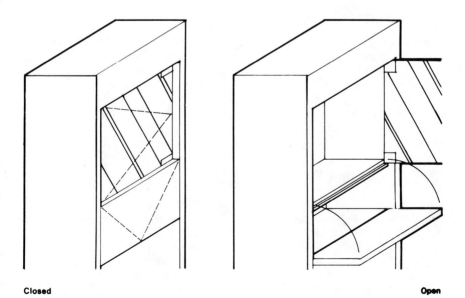

Closed   Open

3-17. Glass swinging doors may be locked with a hinged panel.

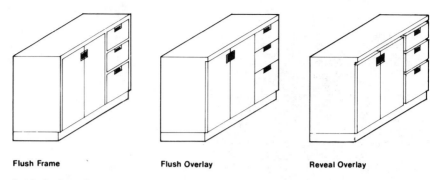

Flush Frame   **Flush Overlay**   **Reveal Overlay**

3-18. Styles of cabinet construction.

tolerances between doors, drawers, and frame, which require precise wood-working to maintain an even gap. Eliminating the face frame saves some material and labor costs.

Flush overlay construction provides a clean, contemporary image. The cabinet frame is not visible unless the doors or drawers are opened. Drawers and doors are located in the same plane, separated by a small gap that creates an almost continuous surface plane.

Reveal overlay construction is similar to flush overlay but provides a half-inch standard reveal between the edges of drawers and doors. Both overlay types are economical, since they are finished with plastic laminate.

DISPLAY COMPONENTS

Many stock components exist that can be used to display merchandise effectively. These include a variety of adjustable brackets and standards for product support. Standards for adjustable brackets are either surface mounted or concealed (fig. 3-19). Both designs are similar and consist of a rear-mounted steel channel with a regular pattern of vertical slots designed to receive and interlock with a bracket. The bracket may be attached and relocated vertically anywhere on the standard. Various attachments, which permit these systems to be used for wood or glass shelves and as hang-rod supports, can be affixed to the end of the bracket. However, because the wall must be furred out so that the standards can be mounted behind the projecting wall, concealed standards are expensive to construct. (Furring is creating a space between the base wall and projecting wall with wood members or metal furring.) In addition, the walls must be blocked properly before the standards are installed; the standards are designed to accommodate reasonably heavy loads, which the wall must also be able to support. Brackets are available in stock designs that, while functional, may not satisfy the designer's aesthetic requirements. If this is the case, custom brackets can be fabricated by combining chrome or brass tubing with a bracket adapter (fig. 3-20).

Adjustable shelving and rod displays may also be developed by using pilaster

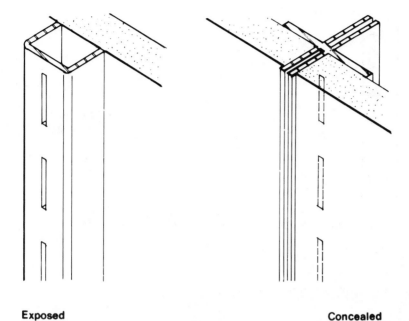

Exposed   Concealed

3-19. Concealed and surface-mounted standards for adjustable brackets.

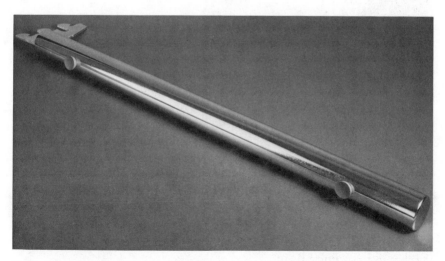

3-20. Adjustable shelf brackets can be custom designed for conventional standards.

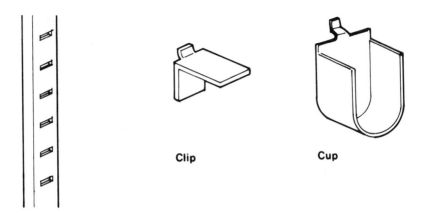

Clip   Cup

3-21. Pilaster standards mount on the sides of vertical surfaces.

3-22. This adjustable slotted hardboard can support a variety of shelf and hook brackets.

standards and brackets (fig. 3-21). These standards mount on the side walls and have small clips that fit into horizontal slots to hold a shelf or a rod. This type of system is typically used inside cabinets or casework with vertical dividers. Other adjustable systems consist of slotted hardboard designed to support a series of different shelf and hook brackets (fig. 3-22). If the stock wall materials are not acceptable to the designer, this type of system can also be custom-built to the desired specifications and requirements.

Stationary hooks and brackets are another option for wall mounting. There are several well-designed lines of colorful plastic products from which to choose. Or, custom brackets can be designed and fabricated relatively inexpensively with chrome or brass and concealed plate mountings. Standard metal tubes and connections can be used to make three-dimensional display grids supported by the floor, wall, or ceiling. Products can be hung from the grid or placed on shelves. This system offers the benefit of flexibility; the displays may be taken down, redesigned, and reconstructed easily to give an area of the store a new look.

The success of any fixture design depends on the correct interpretation of the storeowner's intent, knowledge, and direction. The storeowner should know the best display techniques for the merchandise and suggest these to the designer. The designer must evaluate the owner's direction and the size, weight, and color of the product and accommodate these factors within the fixture. Store fixtures are precisely designed selling machines. In consideration of the store's ever-increasing operating costs, store fixtures must display the product with a minimum of wasted space. Smaller stores, more so than the large ones, will require the designer to be creative in developing display fixtures. In a successful display, every inch is well used.

FOUR

THE STOREFRONT

The front of a retail store serves several functions. First, it acts as a symbol of the store—its merchandise and philosophy. Second, the front is an attraction to draw shoppers to the store. It provides a filter or lens through which the designer can control the shopper's perception of the store; and last, it provides physical transition from the street or mall to the store's interior.

From a distance, the storefront is the singular element of contact between the shopper and the merchant. Therefore, the store's concept and merchandise must be clearly reflected in the design of the storefront, otherwise potential customers may pass by, not understanding the store. Unless the shopper, prompted by advertising or a previous shopping experience, already has the store in mind as a destination, the shopper's interest must be captured. Even if the shopper is willing to try the store because of advertising or other recommendation, he may, upon seeing the storefront for the first time, decline to enter if the front does not fulfill his expectations. For example, if a shopper expects to find a discounted jewelry store but the storefront makes the store seem expensive, the shopper may become intimidated or disappointed and leave.

The storefront must give the shopper an unmistakable impression of the store's price range, product, service, selection, degree of sales assistance, level of quality, and type of shopper the store is attempting to attract. The storefront performs this task through properly selected materials, signs, views to the interior, product displays, and the ease or difficulty of access the entrance provides. The difference between a store with a window display of a few products without visible price tags surrounded by fine marble, as shown in figure 4-1, and a store with a standard storefront system displaying massive amounts of

4-1 and 4-2. Shoppers can sense the operation, pricing, and intended market group of a store simply by viewing the storefront materials, signs, and form.

merchandise behind floor-to-ceiling glass with large paper price signs taped to the glass (fig. 4-2) is evident. With one look at each storefront, the shopper has a complete grasp of the product, price, and type of service each store offers. He can judge whether the store is intended to satisfy his needs and the needs of those like him.

The storefront is an attraction for the shopper. It captures his attention, draws him near, and invites him in to see and purchase the products or services for sale. If the front is properly designed, one quick look will tell the shopper if the store's philosophy is in his interest. But this is not enough, however. The front must be attractive enough to draw all potential buyers. Well-designed stores are a singular attraction. Through a combination of form, materials, lighting, signs, and product display, the designer can create a magnet attracting the proper customers to the storefront (fig. 4-3).

The designer and the display manager have complete control over what passers-by see within the store. The storefront acts both as a filter to screen out store elements the designer does not wish the shopper to see, such as service areas, and as a lens to focus attention on the elements the designer does wish the shopper to see—the products for sale. In the storefront, opaque and transparent surfaces combine with controlled lighting and well-designed product displays to enhance both the product and the store's image.

Finally, the storefront is a transition area between the street or mall and the store itself. This transition space must meet the expectations of the shopper. If a customer expects exclusivity, the transition area must be designed to control the flow of people into the store. If the shopper expects the store to attract the general public, the transition into the store must be easy and open.

STOREFRONT DESIGN

There are three areas of limitation in storefront design: transparency, the plan, and the design statement (fig. 4-4).

Transparency

A storefront elevation design can range from a completely open space, both physically and visually, to one that is completely closed. Open storefronts have no physical elements separating the street or mall from the store proper (fig.

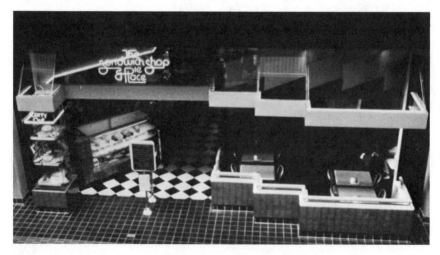

4-3. This storefront incorporates product display, a clear view of the interior, creative sign display, and a defined, stepped-back entrance.

STOREFRONT DESIGN

Transparency	Plan	Design
open	projected	strong
closed	recessed	neutral

4-4. The three major elements of storefront design.

4-5). In effect, there is no front save for a sign band or sign above the storefront opening. This type of storefront can be achieved in an enclosed mall as well as a street environment. Creating a completely open front in an enclosed mall environment is simple because the concerns of weather infiltration are non-existent. Even in a street location, open fronts can be designed. Wet weather conditions can be handled by an overhanging canopy, and interior temperature can be maintained through the use of an air curtain located at the storefront. An air curtain is a continuous source of forced air that flows down at the line of the storefront, thereby creating an invisible barrier to heat transmission.

Open storefronts reached their peak of prominence in the enclosed mall shopping center. In the late 1960s and early 1970s, the use of open storefronts for stores in malls was widespread. Since that time, their popularity has moderated and many shopping malls do not permit them at all. The reasons for this posture are twofold. One, most malls are now designed as a street concept as opposed to a department-store concept. In the street concept, the stores are assembled in a mall as a well-defined group of independent merchants connected only by a neutral, streetlike, enclosed mall passage. Designers of these malls attempt to replicate the feeling of an outdoor shopping street within an interior space. Therefore, the use of open storefronts on such a "street" does not follow tradition and may destroy the image the developer is attempting to create. Many of the earlier enclosed malls were designed in the department-store concept; open storefronts were then both acceptable and encouraged by landlords. These shopping centers had a mall that was more of a department store aisle than a street. Within this aisle, kiosks (island stores) were permitted, creating, in combination with the open storefronts along either side of the

4-5. A completely open storefront encourages browsing and invites passers-by to enter, but lacks a definable image.

mall, an image of one large department store. The second reason that completely open storefronts have declined in popularity is that most totally exposed stores are not as handsome as they could be with some strategically located screening. Storefronts filter out the less attractive areas that inevitably exist in a store, such as sales or storage areas, and the backs of counters and other display fixtures. The last reason for the decline of fully open storefronts is the security problems they pose. The open design makes it very difficult to monitor exits and permits shoplifters a wide, uncontrolled escape route.

The other extreme is the fully closed storefront (fig. 4-6). In theory, this storefront has no visual or physical openings from the mall into the store. The front is a barrier between the mall and the store; show windows are backed, doors are kept closed and constructed of opaque materials. This type of shop is oriented to the destination shopper and provides an exclusive image. Few completely closed fronts are constructed, however, because of the importance of informing the shopper outside the store of the experience he will have inside the store. Most storefronts are designed to be at most, predominantly open or predominantly closed, with only few at the extremes.

Open storefronts offer the greatest ease of entry for browsers and the least opportunity to state the store image, or filter out or feature various store elements. Closed storefronts make it more difficult for the casual shopper to enter, but offer the greatest possibility for image development and for screening or magnifying store elements.

The storefront and store interior are often viewed by shoppers as they walk along the mall or street only a few feet from the front. Thus, passers-by have an oblique view of the store that may last only a few seconds. The storefront must catch the shopper's attention at his first glance. If the front permits a view deep into the store, the shopper's angle of vision will be increased, extending his viewing time as he walks by. This factor should be considered when the elevation is designed. Several methods can be used to achieve an extended view into the store: open-backed showcases; storefront recesses; and glassed-in or open entrances instead of opaque doors. Eliminating front showcases is another way to increase the viewing angle.

The Plan

The plan of a storefront in relation to the building face or *fascia*—the horizontal band above storefront doors and windows, upon which a sign is often placed— above may show the storefront as either projected or recessed as extreme parameters. The most typical storefronts in malls are aligned flush with the fascia above. Although many street shops have projecting elements, such as bays or awnings, projecting storefronts were, for many years, not constructed in enclosed shopping malls. This is changing rapidly, however. Over the years,

4-6. Because it presents an image of exclusivity and hides the store interior, the completely closed storefront is oriented to the destination shopper, not to casual passers-by.

developers of enclosed malls have become concerned about the sameness of the design of mall stores. Most merchants had built their storefronts right on the lease line in order to use every bit of their expensive leased space. Consequently, the basic differences among storefront designs had been limited to differences in materials and in the amount of storefront transparency. Storefronts had become very two-dimensional. To increase the use of three-dimensional designs and offer greater design variety (and also lease more area within a given space), the concept of projected storefronts was developed for use in enclosed malls. Most new or remodeled malls now permit projected storefronts. To achieve this end, the tenants' leasable area includes a three- to four-foot rectangle of space in front of their store, into which elements of their storefront may project. There are many different methods of projecting the storefront, the most common of which are display bays, awnings and canopies, and glass greenhouselike projecting elements (fig. 4-7).

Recessed storefronts are common in the traditional street stores and also in enclosed malls (fig. 4-8). Recessed storefront areas in the traditional retail street were designed to display merchandise away from the glare of the sun; to permit shoppers to look into the store from an area protected from the weather; and ultimately to draw the customer into the store. In almost all cases, these reasons for recessing are not valid for retail stores in an enclosed mall. Lighting is usually controlled by the mall architecture to shield the storefront from direct sunlight and the weather factor is eliminated by the enclosed location. The only traditional reason to use a recessed front is to draw the shopper into the store, by easing the physical transition from mall to store. Major storefront recesses usually contain significant product displays; the intention is for the shopper to be sold on the front product, follow the line of product into the storefront recess, and then be drawn into the store proper. Minor storefront recesses may be used to give a three-dimensional quality to storefronts even if projecting storefronts are not permitted or possible. With minor recesses, bays can be formed, entrances can be emphasized, the entire front can be recessed, and a canopy placed overall, extending to the building or lease line.

The Design Statement

The design statement or look of a storefront is the identifiable pattern formed by all the design elements. These patterns might be labeled traditional, modern, Cape Cod, greenhouse, or postmodern, for example. The design statement depends on a myriad of factors, including the overall store concept, the product for sale, and the location of the store.

First, it is important that the storefront design reflect the entire store. Store designs are best when they are consistent, integrating details, materials, and colors inside the store with the storefront. The shopper should be able to anticipate the design of the store interior after seeing its outside. In addition, the design statement should be one that will be fashionable throughout the tenure of the store lease. Retail store designs are subject to rapid changes in trends and fashion. Both the public and the retail industry view an outdated store with definite derision. Design trends move quickly. The greenhouse look may be in style for several years, then may be out. Similarly, stained glass, high-

4-7. Projected storefronts add variety to rows of shopping-mall stores and increase the variety of possible design expressions.

4-8. Recessed storefronts protect shoppers from the weather, shield merchandise from the sun, and draw customers into the store.

tech, postmodern, and barnwood looks may come and go. The designer has several choices: he may attempt to break new ground by establishing a new look; he may ride the crest of a design wave that he hopes will last as long as the lease term of the store; he may use a very traditional design, such as Victorian; or he may work with traditional materials in a neutral, undefinable manner. To a great degree, the length of time that a design is likely to remain fashionable relates to the intensity of the design statement. If the design is entirely neutral, it cannot go out of fashion since it has no fashion. If the design statement is very strong, the risk that it may fall out of fashion is increased.

Any design concept may become a strong or a neutral statement. A design can allude, with selected materials and geometric forms, to the Hall of Mirrors at Versailles or can attempt to replicate it. A general guideline for developing the design statement is to establish a strong design only if the product itself is a weak sensory experience and will not have significant impact (fig. 4-9). If the product has something to say, it should become the most important element of a storefront and store design statement (fig. 4-10). Most products will provide a great sensory experience if properly displayed, so the design statement of most storefronts should be more neutral than strong. The strategy is simple: sell the product, not the storefront. In most cases, this strategy will work. However, if the product involved is insurance, for example, then it is very difficult to sell the product and a strong design statement will be necessary. If the product has a strong olfactory but limited visual impact, such as prepared food, the smell of the product should be sold (within the limits of any lease agreements regarding odors) along with a strong design statement. A moderate design statement might be appropriate for products that are common, not visually overwhelming, and cannot be grouped to form a strong visual statement, such as cosmetics.

STOREFRONT ELEMENTS

Whether the architecture of a storefront can be classified as neutral or strong, three basic elements are present in every well-designed storefront: display, transitional, and identification elements.

Display Elements

The display elements of the storefront permit the shopper to see the merchandise for sale under the best possible conditions. Products may be displayed at the storefront in built-in show windows that are part of the storefront construction or in store fixtures placed against a storefront window or opening. Show windows may be constructed with or without backs. If unbacked, the show window will permit the shopper to see beyond the displayed merchandise to the store; if backed, the show window will focus the customer's complete attention on the displayed product.

The smaller the product, the more likely it will have to be displayed very close to the storefront. Most jewelry, for example, must be displayed in the storefront, whereas larger products, such as furniture, may be effectively displayed away from the storefront. The focus of storefront displays should be

4-9. A strong storefront design statement can be used to unify the merchandise displayed or provide visual impact lacking in the merchandise.

4-10. A neutral storefront design statement allows the product to become the major visual statement.

approximately at eye level to be most effective, but the elevation of a feature storefront display should relate to the height at which the product is typically viewed—that is, hats should be displayed slightly above eye level, shoes substantially below.

The designer must determine which product, if any, will be featured in the storefront. The importance of displaying these products must be weighed against the shopper's need, as he stands outside the store, to know what is inside. Shoppers want to know what to expect upon entering the store; without this knowledge, they may be unsure and choose not to enter. Because their merchandise is so small, jewelry stores, for example, should display their merchandise directly at the storefront. However, it may be equally important for the storefront to offer a view into the store, to indicate the store's overall size, layout, selection, and services. To solve this problem, storefront jewelry may be displayed in unbacked showcases, or viewing windows adjacent to the show windows may be provided (fig. 4-11).

Not all stores require storefront display showcases. It may be entirely appropriate simply to enclose the entire storefront with clear glazing, giving passers-by an unhindered view of all store merchandise and the store layout. In this approach, products may be displayed in changeable, temporary displays at the storefront glazing without significantly reducing the view into the store. The storefront should provide a suitable frame for the merchandise of the store, either one large frame to enclose the view of the store and all its merchandise or several smaller frames to accentuate feature displays at the storefront. In

4-11. This storefront displays small products at eye level and gives the shopper a clear view into the store.

either case the frames should have forms, colors, and materials that relate conceptually to the product sold and focus the shopper's attention on the product. The storefront frame should not compete with the product. As a modern print would not be displayed in a baroque frame, the latest in video equipment, with its crisp machined metal and smoothly formed plastic parts, should not be framed with heavy, rough-hewn, timber and stained glass. Both the modern print and video equipment should have a simple, neutral frame of glass and metal or plastic. The store frame should also be well detailed, for poorly designed or executed details detract from the product displayed. Ideally, the materials and forms of the storefront should relate to the overall design of the store and provide a visual and physical transition into the store.

Storefront lighting for product display is critical. The key rule requires lighting at the storefront to illuminate something important. This object to be illuminated will most likely be the product; it may be a sign; or it might be the storefront itself, if a strong design statement is required. But it will not be the floor. Designers often place high-intensity lighting aimed at the floor of the storefront. This detracts from the show window as well as the product displays by drawing the shopper's eyes away from the product. In most cases, the product at the storefront should be brightly illuminated and the lighting system should be flexible. Depending on the requirements of the display, this system may include track lights, adjustable recessed lights, and fixed lighting, as well as lighting from above, below, to either side, or from the front or back. Show window designers use many effects to attract shoppers to the window. Exceptionally bright lights are very attention-getting, as are light fixtures with colored filters, which can be used to create unusual product display effects. Storefront display lighting must be flexible so that it may accommodate changes in the types and styles of product to be displayed there. A few rules of lighting should be observed as well. Storefront lighting should not spill out into the mall and light sources (direct glare) should not be visible. Light should not fall on the storefront glazing; if light is directed toward the glass, it will become visible and act as a barrier between the shopper and the store. If the store is outdoors or even in some indoor locations, direct sunlight may fall upon storefront glazing and create glare and reflections. To eliminate this problem, a canopy or awning should be provided or the glazing should be recessed from the path of sunlight. Storefront display areas should have a flexible system of hanging display from the storefront ceiling or soffit and should have at least one duplex electrical outlet box at each show window or display area.

The security of storefront displays must also be considered. Shoplifting is one of the shortcomings of a totally open storefront; products that are easy to grab will unfortunately be stolen. Protecting merchandise in an open storefront often becomes more expensive than the cost of constructing a closed store. Shoplifters are rewarded by poorly secured storefront merchandise; they can grab merchandise and be on their way without even entering the store. Thieves can reach around an unbacked, open display case or hook small items such as jewelry through the unsealed joint between lights of frameless glass. The battle between the shoplifter and the storeowner is ceaseless and the designer should provide as much forethought about security as possible. Electric devices and methods can be incorporated within the storefront to announce a person entering the store or to indicate the unauthorized removal of products, as discussed in chapter 7. These devices, coupled with secure displays and well-located cash counters or desks, will decrease shoplifting.

Transitional Elements

Transitional elements in a storefront are the forms and materials, such as doors, gates, grilles, and arches, that define the passageway between the street or mall and the store interior. While these elements and their effects may be subtle, they are nevertheless important. Transitions help develop store identity, help create a sense of commitment to the store in the shopper's mind, and also announce the entrance of the store. The shopper must be aware that he is entering a store if he is to establish a relationship with the store, to identify and remember it. Imagine an enclosed mall filled entirely with open storefronts. A shopper would move from store to store with no sense of transition. In these conditions, his recollection of shopping would be a blur even if he made purchases. To establish identity, storefronts must create a tangible sense of transition. Moreover, identification and recall enable the shopper to return and to advertise the store through word-of-mouth recommendation. Transition areas also create a sense of commitment in the mind of the shopper. When he enters the store (and a good transition element will give him this feeling of entrance), the customer subconsciously makes a commitment. It may not be a commitment to purchase something, but it might be strong enough to make him look seriously at the merchandise. Even a slight shopper commitment is better than none. Some people even feel compelled to buy something once they have entered a store, although this level of commitment is probably rare.

The transition may be subtle, such as a change of flooring, wall, or ceiling material from mall to store. Or it may be a change in geometric form, such as a drop in the ceiling or the placement of solid entrance elements in an otherwise transparent storefront (fig. 4-12). Traditional entrance forms include the arch,

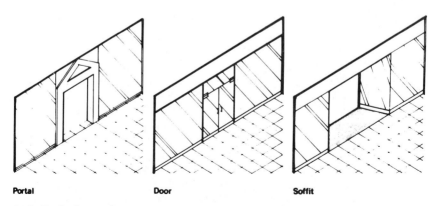

Portal   Door   Soffit

4-12. Typical storefront transitional elements.

post-and-beam, and pediment openings; derivatives of these forms are commonly used to mark the retail-store entrances. A swinging door alone will create a definite sense of transition in the shopper's mind. Entrances that are open and require no physical effort from the shopper to enter need some form of architectural treatment to announce the transition. While transitional elements are important in a storefront design, the transition should not become a forbidding barrier for the shopper. After all, the major point of the storefront is to invite the shopper into the store.

Identification Elements

Identification elements cause the shopper to recognize, remember, or identify a storefront even if he has never been in the store. The most common identification element is the sign that depicts the store's name and logo. Landlords of most shopping centers, enclosed and strip, restrict the placement of signs. For many years, as a reaction to the overzealous sign designs of some tenants, signs were restricted to a single fascia above the store entrance and the choice of sign technique for use in a given mall was usually very limited. Recently the trend has been toward more freedom in the placement and style of merchant signs. In many enclosed malls, merchants are now restricted only to using quality materials within a limited total sign area. Previous restrictions of sign length, letter height, position within the storefront, and letter type are being dropped in favor of encouraging sign design creativity and diversity. There has been a resurgence of neon signs, and a development of sophisticated back-lighted box signs, sculptural, minimal, blade, and many other sign variations. For retail stores located on a street, local sign ordinances may be the controlling factor limiting the sign design. These vary greatly from jurisdiction to jurisdiction, but are usually more concerned with size than location or technique.

Since signs in many malls have been limited to the name of the store, with regulations often prohibiting signs from listing the items for sale, prices, or any other promotional material, signs have become less significant as a device to draw shoppers into the store. For this reason, store signs have frequently become only a graphic symbol to be recognized and remembered. Some retailers have become very sophisticated and confident and have reduced front signs to minimal proportions. Successful symbols may even be unreadable. Many retailers strive to use the same symbol consistently throughout all their advertising and packaging. The store sign must, therefore, be easy to recognize as the store symbol. Ideally, its letter style and look will match the printed symbol that appears on store packaging and advertising. In general, the more often the symbol is used, the more important it becomes. A tenant with a national chain of stores, then, will be more concerned about sign clarity and consistency of graphic display than the single storeowner tenant, who may be inclined to use a more obscure or minimal sign since the sign's symbol has limited exposure.

In many cases, the sign takes a back seat to the storefront, the product, and the overall image of the store as an identification element. Mrs. Field's Cookies' red awnings, Crate and Barrel's overall design, and McDonald's arches are at least as important as their signs in terms of store identification.

Glazing

Storefront glazing may be used as an entrance, window, or finishing material. Although glazing is usually transparent, it may become noticeable if it is improperly designed or installed. Poorly detailed glass, glass subject to reflections, wavy glass, or dirty glass will impede the shopper's view of the store. Properly installed and maintained glass, on the other hand, attracts customers with its crispness and sparkle.

Exterior glass panels and the framing methods to be used must be analyzed in terms of wind load. This analysis should be performed by an architect or structural engineer. Some manufacturers of storefront glass and metal systems have developed wind-load tables for their systems, which can be used by the designer to create a storefront that will withstand local wind conditions. For indoor locations, glass size may be dictated by transporting concerns: door and elevator sizes, along with other interior elements that might block the passage of glass from the truck to the installation site, must be considered.

Exposed glass edges should be ground, whereas edges that will be framed need not be ground. Ground edges take two forms, either a pencil edge (rounded) or an arris edge (chamfered) (fig. 4-13). Glass may be sandblasted or acid-etched for different graphic effects. Clear glass may be spray-painted any color on the back, to create opaque colored glass. Glass may also be patterned rather than polished, if opaque, geometrically patterned glass is desired.

Safety glass is glass that has been treated or processed so that it either resists breaking or breaks, upon impact, into small granules rather than large, jagged shards, to reduce the possibility of physical harm. Tempered and laminated glass, discussed below, are both forms of clear safety glass. Safety glass is used in hazardous locations, which include all heavily trafficked areas and any place where there is a high risk of impact. Federal regulations stipulate that all glass doors, sidelights adjacent to doors, and glass less than 18 inches from the ground must be made of safety glass. The designer of a storefront may be wise to consider using safety glass in most public areas as relatively inexpensive, permanent insurance against harm to customers.

Float glass is the glass typically used in most construction. It has replaced plate glass, which is no longer manufactured. When ordering float glass, the designer must specify whether clear or tinted glass is desired. Tinted glass is not recommended for retail storefronts, however, as it reduces the customer's

4-13. Two types of ground glass edges: at left, the rounded pencil edge; at right, the chamfered arris edge.

view of the merchandise and affects color perception. Typically ¼-inch float glass is used for framed interior glass.

Tempered glass, a safety glass, is a heat-strengthened float glass that is many times more resistant to impact breakage than untreated float glass is. Tempered glass may be used in a storefront without mullions—that is, framed only at top and bottom. In this type of frameless installation, ½-inch glass is generally used, although ⅜- and ¼-inch glass may be used on smaller panels. If thinner glazing (⅜ or ¼ inch thick) is used, it may be necessary to fill the joint between the panels of glass with clear silicone, to maintain proper alignment between glass panels and reduce waviness in the glass. Unless the installation must be weatherproof, the joints of ½-inch frameless glass need not be sealed with silicone. Large panels (in excess of 12 feet) of tempered glass are available, but only certain American manufacturers are capable of producing these sizes. Therefore, additional construction time and cost will be involved unless one of these special manufacturers is located near the project area (which would result in lower shipping costs). Smaller panels of glass can usually be tempered locally.

Tempered glass cannot be reworked after it has been tempered. All edges must be ground, all holes or notches cut, and the glass panel must be cut to the exact size of the opening before it enters the oven. This means that tempered glass cannot be ordered until the major framing elements of the storefront are in place and opening sizes can be measured. Storefront-size sections of curved glass cannot be tempered, as the equipment needed simply does not now exist. Technology in this area is advancing rapidly, however, and such curved sections may soon be available. Tempered glass is also subject to spontaneous breakage. On rare occasions, glass panels will virtually explode and disintegrate without warning. The reason for this spontaneous breakage is not known, but it does not present any substantial hazard to the public unless tempered glass is placed overhead.

There are two methods of treating glass and in both cases, the glass is placed in a heat-treating oven. In one, the glass is held in place in the oven, gripped with tongs at the top. This process leaves tong marks in the finished product and also causes a more uneven glass panel to be produced, since the glass bends, stretches, and curls within the oven. The unevenness caused by this process is generally not a problem in smaller panels of glass. Tong marks are a problem only for glass that will not be framed. Where the edges are to be exposed, the designer must specify that tong marks be located at the top or bottom and buried in the frame; if edges are to be exposed, the float method of tempering should be specified, which produces a superior product. With this method, the glass is floated within the oven on a current of air. No tong marks are produced and the glass does not distort in the oven, since it is heated more evenly as it is strengthened.

Laminated glass consists of two or more panels of float glass with a plastic sheet or sheets bonded between the panels. Laminated glass is a safety glass that is substantially weaker than tempered glass, but has its own special breakage feature: upon impact, laminated glass will break but the plastic sheet within holds the panel together. This makes laminated glass especially suitable for overhead glassed areas. Laminated glass may also be curved in sizes suitable for use in storefronts, although this is an expensive process. Unlike tempered glass, laminated glass may be cut or ground after lamination.

Glass block is a glass material that is laid like masonry. It may be used in a storefront to provide a translucent, decorative, solid barrier. Glass blocks are available in several sizes and in clear or opaque finishes, as well as finishes that are reflective during the day and transparent at night. Glass block is an expensive but interesting glazing material, not suitable for display use.

Closures

Sliding doors may be made of opaque materials like wood or metal, as see-through grilles, or as glass doors. Sliding doors either hang from an overhead track or rest in a bottom track. Rollers are located in the bottom or top track and the doors slide to one side or the other along the tracks. Sliding doors may be biparting—separating in the middle—or slide in one direction only. Panels may slide behind each other, or separate into pockets recessed into the storefront. If a large opening is to be accommodated, however, the stacking space and resulting pocket construction required for the panels could become objectionable, as it would take up expensive floor and storefront space.

Sliding glass storefront sections are generally constructed of tempered glass and aluminum framing sections. Standardized framing systems are available that consist of variously shaped and sized aluminum components. Aluminum finishes can be obtained in anodized black; light, medium, or dark bronze; and clear. Baked-on paint finishes may also be applied at the factory to create almost any color. Frameless sliding storefront sections are also available that consist of top and bottom aluminum rails, containing the rollers or guides, that hold in place ½-inch-thick sections of tempered glass (fig. 4-14). The top rail of these panels may be concealed in a soffit to enhance the frameless look. Frameless sliding doors are available in sizes of up to 12 feet if bottom rollers are used to support the door; top-hung doors are available only in smaller sizes. Locks in frameless sliding doors are placed in the bottom rail, which is an inconvenient position for opening and may be difficult for elderly or hand-icapped employees to handle. Frameless sliding door installations are not weatherproof, however, and may be used only indoors. In addition, sections of glass will gap when the door is closed, inviting thieves to hook merchandise through the opening. Moreover, sliding doors cannot be used as fire exits unless they remain open during store hours; since they must remain open all day, they are useful only in enclosed malls or other places with regulated temperatures.

Swinging doors may be made of solid or transparent materials or grilles. Swinging doors give the storeowner the option of keeping the door open or letting it be opened by the shopper. The swinging feature enhances the sense of transition into the store and cuts off street noise or other objectionable environmental conditions outside the store.

Swinging glass doors may be framed in aluminum sections of narrow or wide profile. Frameless ½-inch tempered glass panels with top and bottom rails or bottom rails and top hinge patterns may also be constructed as doors. When

4-14. Frameless tempered-glass panels may be used as sliding doors. The installation shown is twelve feet high.

top hinge patches are used, unframed glazed transom panels may be placed over the door to create an all-glass, mullionless front. Frameless swinging glass doors may be constructed as much as 12 feet high, but doors in constant use should not be higher than 8 feet.

Swinging entrance doors are normally hinged at the top and bottom with pivot hinges rather than leaf hinges. Doors may be offset or center-pivoted depending on the situation. Closers with hold-open features are typically used on swinging doors; in the better installations, such closers are concealed either in the floor or overhead. If the closer is to be concealed overhead in aluminum framing tube, it must be center-pivoted. Closers may be set to hold doors open from 90 degrees to 180 degrees. If 180-degree swing is desired, offset pivots and closers must be used.

Sometimes it is desirable to install a swinging door in the face of a storefront that will not provide public access, such as a door serving an office or storeroom. In this situation, a concealed door is required and it is possible to design a door that is unnoticeable to all but the most observant passers-by. In this fashion, the store's service requirements may be handled, but not at the expense of the storefront design (fig. 4-15).

Overhead security closures include overhead rolling doors and grilles. Overhead rolling doors are composed of interlocking aluminum slats that may be rolled into a coil and stored above the ceiling or pulled down on side tracks to create a solid door. Tracks are mounted to solid structural surfaces or to steel tubes that extend from the floor to the structure above (fig. 4-16). These

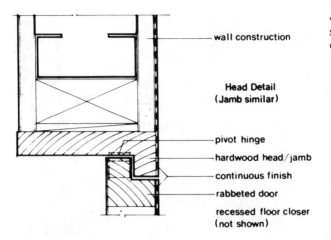

4-15. Horizontal section of a concealed door.

wall construction

Head Detail
(Jamb similar)

pivot hinge

hardwood head/jamb

continuous finish

rabbeted door

recessed floor closer
(not shown)

doors are available in anodized aluminum finishes and may be finished with paint. Sometimes the door is constructed of unfinished mill aluminum but the tracks and bottom rail of the door are anodized to enhance the appearance of the storefront during the day. Overhead grilles also roll on tracks, but are composed of round horizontal bars joined and separated by vertical links in a grid pattern (fig. 4-17). When closed, grille doors do not block air circulation or the view of the store, but do offer security. In addition, grilles are usually less expensive than rolling doors.

Overhead closures do not squander valuable floor area, since they require only a small space for the side tracks and the bottom rail. Overhead rolling doors and grilles are usually installed in stores located in shopping malls, since

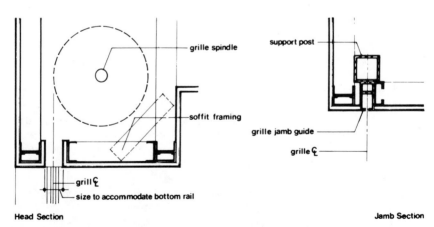

grille spindle

support post

soffit framing

grille jamb guide

grille ₵

grill ₵

size to accommodate bottom rail

Head Section

Jamb Section

4-16. Vertical and horizontal sections of typical overhead door and grille construction.

4-17. An overhead rolling grille closure. *(Miller Stockman, Palm Desert, CA; photo courtesy of Atlas Door Corporation)*

the doors remain open during the hours of store operation and provide no weather protection. Some jurisdictions require exit doors to be placed in grilles or doors, to permit emergency egress when the overhead door is pulled down. Other regulations require the door to be manually operable from the inside as well as automatically operable, to accommodate the needs of any employees who remain in the store after business hours.

Overhead doors are either manually or electrically operated. However, doors more than 10 feet wide should be electrically operated so that they do not overwhelm store employees. Two control panels that operate the motorized door are necessary; one panel outside the store and one panel inside the store. Both panels are usually located near the storefront. These controls are keyed to provide security. Metal enclosures to house the rolled-up grille may be purchased for overhead doors, although this enclosure is usually not necessary. It is generally a requirement, however, that grilles be enclosed with a fire-rated gypsum board and metal stud barrier. Access panels must then be provided at appropriate locations to service the enclosed door and its motor.

Side closures include side-coiling or accordion-folding grilles. Side-coiling grilles operate like overhead coiling grilles, except that the coil is placed at the side of the storefront rather than overhead, and the grille slides along overhead and bottom tracks. Side-coiling grilles are usually motorized and require only a minimum of floor space. Side-folding accordion grilles are similar to side-coiling grilles but fold into a pattern approximately 8 inches wide instead of coiling when opened. They slide along a top track and are pulled or pushed manually. Pockets must be created within the storefront architecture to accommodate the door when it is open. Accordion grilles are less expensive than coiling grilles; both types are available in the same variety of finishes as overhead grilles.

Finishing Materials

Many different finishing materials may be used in storefront construction to frame the storefront openings, provide a sign background, or create a solid surface. The key quality desired in any material used for this purpose is durability, since the storefront receives intense physical contact from shoppers and cleaning personnel. Appropriate materials that can take abuse are metal, hardwood, glass, tile, brick, and stone. Other possible materials are plaster or integral-color plastic laminate on particleboard. Plastic sheets, exposed gypsum board, or softwood may be used for areas that are not subject to physical contact, such as sign backgrounds. A durable material such as metal, stone, or tile should always be provided for the base of the storefront, since this area is subject to constant kicking and contact with floor-cleaning equipment.

SIGNS

Signs for retail stores are usually custom-designed and fabricated to the letter style, size, and material requirements of the tenant. There are two basic types of signs: individual letter signs and panel signs. Both types of signs may be either internally or externally illuminated (fig. 4-18).

Individual Letter Signs

Individual, nonilluminated letter signs may be constructed of many materials, but the most common are wood, plastic, or metal. The individual letters may be saw-cut from sheet material, or, in the case of plastic or metal, formed or cast into shapes. Saw-cut wood letters are usually ¾ to 1 inch thick, while saw-cut plastic and metal letters may range from ¼ to ½ inch thick. Formed or cast letters can be made to any practical thickness. Wood letters may be painted a color or stained and clear finished. Plastic letters have integral color. Metal letters may be painted, anodized aluminum, or the base metal may be exposed, such as bronze or brass. Individual, nonilluminated letters may be mounted directly to and flush with the background surface or set away from the wall on pins. Pin mounting is useful if the sign background surface is an irregular material, such as brick or stucco. Sign letters may also be pin mounted on smooth background surfaces to achieve a floating effect.

Nonilluminated individual letters also include painted gold or silver-leaf letters, other painted letters, and "nondimensional" or very thin die-cut letters, which are usually applied directly to storefront glass (fig. 4-19). The size and

Individual Letters Non Illuminated

Panel Sign Non Illuminated

Individual Letters Silhouette Illuminated

Individual Letters Neon Illuminated

Individual Letters Illuminated Translucent Face

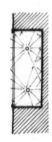

Panel Sign Illuminated

4-18. Typical retail storefront signs.

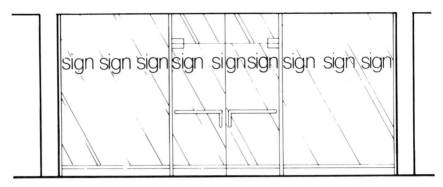

4-19. Repeated decal signs, where permitted, provide an interesting design alternative.

placement of decal letters are frequently restricted by shopping-center owners. Lettering is typically set adjacent to doors at eye level to provide easy store identification. Small (3 to 4 inch) "nondimensional" letters are also effective if repeated in a pattern just below eye level. In some cases, this serves the dual purpose of identifying the store and helping shoppers avoid walking into the storefront glazing. Individual nonilluminated letters may be floodlit or silhouetted in front of an illuminated surface, such as storefront glazing, or sandblasted or etched into the storefront glazing.

Individual, illuminated letter signs include those with translucent faces, silhouette type, and exposed neon letters. Translucent-face sign letters are at least 8 inches high and typically fabricated from sheet metal or cast metal for the letter frame and translucent plastic for the face of the letter. Inside the letter, a cold cathode tube (fluorescent lamp) is bent and fitted to the shape of the letter; the back of the letter is sealed with metal. The translucent plastic face is available in many colors; many shades of white can be obtained from the cold cathode lamp as well. Translucent-face letters are usually mounted directly to a sign background without pins. Electrical ballasts for the sign, junction boxes, and disconnect must be concealed behind the sign background and these will require access panels for servicing.

Silhouette signs are composed of individual letters that are channel sectioned, die-cast, or made of sheet metal, then pin mounted about 2 inches away from the background surface. Cold cathode tube lighting is placed in each letter and the light from this tube bounces off the background, providing a halo effect for each letter. The letters are readable in silhouette under low or night lighting conditions. The effectiveness of silhouette signs depends on the reflectivity of the background material. The greater the reflection, the greater the contrast between the sign surface and the background. However, too much reflection (such as a mirrored surface) is not desirable since it may reflect the lamps within the sign instead of the sign itself. The minimum height for silhouette and translucent-face letters is about 8 inches because of the limitations of forming and placing the cold cathode tubes. Fasteners, attachments, and all electrical devices for translucent-face and silhouette signs should be concealed. Manufacturers, underwriters, or union labels should not be exposed to view.

Neon signs are the third type of illuminated, individual letter signs (fig. 4-20). Neon is a colorless, chemically inert gas that glows reddish-orange when placed inside a sealed glass tube and charged with electric current. Neon tubes are of thin diameter and, unlike cold cathode tubes, are not coated inside with phosphor. Other gases, such as argon, helium, krypton, and xenon, may be used alone or mixed with neon to produce other colors. The inside of the glass tube can also be coated with a translucent color. Neon signs are very playful and creative, since the glass tubing can be bent in many different shapes and used for signature and pictorial graphics as well as simple letter forms. Neon signs may be set in front of an opaque or behind a clear glass sign background—either method is very effective. However, protection for neon signs must be considered, as the glass tubes are very fragile and easily broken. It is desirable to place the signs behind a glass or clear plastic protective shield or to make the sign unreachable. Neon signs require transformed electrical power, and consideration also must be given to the concealment and access requirements of remotely located transformers.

4-20. Neon signs can be attractively combined with clear-plastic panel signs.
(Architect: LUBOTSKY, METTER, WORTHINGTON + LAW, LTD.;
photography: Karant & Associates, Inc.)

Panel Signs

Panel signs are constructed as a flat panel rather than as separate letters. These signs, in effect, provide both the sign letter and the background in one package. The background material and the foreground letters may be clear, translucent, or opaque. The letters may be painted, silkscreened, added as decals, or etched on the background surface, or they may be thin (¼ inch or less) individual letters cut from wood, plastic, or metal and adhered to the background surface. The letters may also be cut out of the panel to form a negative image.

Panel signs may be made of any material. If illuminated, the panel is often made of plastic with letters painted on the surface or all of the surface except the letters painted to create a negative image. Fluorescent tubes are located behind the panel and this light passes through the face to reveal the letter. A similar sign may be created by sandblasting the sign letters into mirrored glass. The sandblasting removes the silvering from the mirror back and permits light to pass through the now-translucent glass surface.

Nonilluminated panel signs may be affixed directly to the storefront surface, placed on pins, or hung like a picture. If the panel sign is illuminated, it is called a box sign. Box signs may be surface mounted (prohibited in most malls) or recessed. If recessed, box signs can be carefully integrated into a

4-21. Blade signs simplify store identification.

storefront to create a very subtle and distinctive sign. Because virtually any pattern may be etched or silkscreened onto the background surface, panel signs offer the designer the greatest freedom of expression. The sign is not limited only to letters, but may incorporate pictorial or abstract designs, which provide illuminated works of art as well as store identification.

Sign Location

Shopping-center developers, in their quest to control external store signs, required for many years that signs be located in a fascia band above the doors and the display windows of a store. In many cases, this has been a logical location for store signs: the signs are high enough to be seen from a distance; they are not obscured by shoppers standing in front of the store; they do not block the view inside the store; and they are placed in an otherwise unimportant part of the storefront. Unfortunately, the imposition of sign-location requirements by developers across the country has created a boring sameness in the signs of many shopping malls. Recently, developers have begun to encourage merchants to be more creative in sign design and location. Some malls now permit signs in any part of the storefront. Many shopping areas also permit and encourage locations other than signs attached parallel to the storefront, such as blade and accessory signs. Blade signs, as shown in fig. 4-21, are located perpendicular to the storefront and are particularly useful in narrow malls, where it is difficult for the shopper to see signs parallel to the storefront. Accessory signs include eye-level signs on storefront glass adjacent to doors; signs inlaid in floor tiling; and three-dimensional or other signs and symbols hung from the soffit above an entrance door.

Since most storefront signs are very expensive, the designer should maintain an open mind about signs and work to create signs that are effective as store identification and memorable in their location, design, and construction. A successful store sign can favorably separate one storefront design from the multitude of other storefronts in a mall.

FIVE

MATERIALS

Materials used in retail stores may be categorized by the basic space-defining elements they cover or form, such as materials for floors, walls, and ceilings. The general criteria for selecting a material are its image, physical properties, and cost.

The image of a material depends to a great degree on its inherent qualities, its traditional use, and the context in which the designer presents it. For example, although finished natural wood connotes warmth, richness, and quality, its image may be enhanced or altered by the context in which it is presented. Finished, natural wood illuminated with incandescent lighting and placed near polished marble or granite will have an enhanced image of warmth and richness. If, on the other hand, it is presented in a room with cool white fluorescent lighting and a concrete floor, the natural wood will take on a different image. The image of a material is, therefore, determined by its relationship to other materials as well as its inherent qualities.

The designer must also consider the material's physical properties—how it absorbs sound and light; surface texture, hardness, color, and pattern; smell; durability; and structure. In addition, most finish materials have test ratings for combustibility, flame, and smoke; the designer must determine compliance with codes for each material and test category. All store materials should be durable, fashionable, and cleanable or easy to replace. The requirement for durability is dictated by location and use. If the material is out of reach and not subject to regular wear, such as a ceiling, the need for durability is lessened.

Last, the designer must consider the cost of a material. The cost must be analyzed in terms of first cost and cost over the lease term for the store. Some materials, such as wall paint, have an inexpensive first cost, but must be redone on a regular basis over the term of the lease. The resulting cost should reflect not only the cost of repainting, but the disruption this work will have on an operating store.

FLOORS

Carpeting

Carpeting is the most popular flooring material in retail stores for four major reasons: it is relatively inexpensive; it is available in a wide variety of colors and textures; it is comfortable to walk on; and it has significant sound-absorption properties.

The average life of retail-store carpeting is about eight years, so a store should be designed to facilitate carpet removal and replacement. Carpet replacement should not necessitate relocating permanent store fixtures for its accomplishment. Therefore, the carpet should run up to but not beneath permanent fixtures, or a different hard surface material, such as tile or hardwood, should be placed beneath the fixture and form a border around it. Carpets may be installed permanently, wall to wall, or as a freestanding rug over or inlaid into a hard surface material. Carpet tiles may also be used where access to the floor underneath is required or where selective replacement may be necessary, as in high-traffic areas (carpet tiles are either laid loose or are self-adhering).

There are two basic types of permanent installation, the stretch-in tackless and glue-down methods. In tackless installations, carpets are usually stretched over a pad and held in place by attachment strips nailed into the floor at the perimeter of the carpet. This type of heavily padded installation is used where traffic conditions are light to moderate and where comfort and luxury are necessary. Firm padding such as hair jute must be used in tackless installations to prevent carpet backings from stretching and wrinkling. The padding reduces carpet wear, absorbs sound, and is more comfortable underfoot. Glue-down installations are used where traffic will be moderate to heavy or where hand-cart traffic or other severe conditions will exist. Gluing the carpet to the floor is generally necessary where large, open expanses of floor area must be covered; large areas of carpet will tend to crawl and bunch unless they are glued down.

Most commercial carpeting fiber is nylon. Nylon fibers are synthetic and produce durable, attractive, and cost-efficient carpets. Nylon is available in a wide variety of colors, surface textures, and densities, and with soil, stain, and static resistance. Acrylic-fiber carpets are also used successfully in retail stores. These fibers are similar to wool in appearance, but are not as abrasion-resistant as nylon is. Acrylic fibers must either be blended with nylon or manufactured in a very dense, tight pattern to maintain performance. Other synthetic fibers, such as olefin and polyester, are available as well. In the past, polyester and olefin carpets were generally not selected by designers for retail installations because of fiber limitations in performance or color. Recently, however, technological improvements have produced a spun-yarn look in olefin fibers. New pigments and chemicals, too, have reduced the shine of synthetic carpets and increased the number of colors available. Olefin is less expensive than nylon, yet has most of nylon's properties. Wool carpeting, although attractive and durable, is prohibitively expensive for use in the majority of retail stores.

Carpet density is a prime factor of the durability or performance of a carpet under store traffic conditions. Density is related to the amount of carpet fiber in a given volume of carpet, and is different from carpet weight, which is expressed in ounces per square yard. Density is a factor of pile height and the weight of pile fibers; the greater the weight and the lower the pile height, the greater the density. Therefore, a heavier carpet may be less dense than a lighter carpet if the lighter carpet has a lower pile height. The best performing carpets have low pile height and the most weight per square yard, which yields the highest density. Densities in excess of 4,000 ounces per cubic yard are desirable for carpets used in retail stores.

Carpet comes in two different styles of pile, loop or cut (fig. 5-1). Loop pile consists of uncut loops; cut pile has cut loops. Although both styles of carpeting are acceptable for use in retail stores, the longer length cut-pile carpets, commonly known as plush, do not wear well and are not recommended for commercial use.

The color of the carpeting should be based upon maintenance as well as design considerations. The carpet should be neither too light nor too dark. Since footprints and other dirt can be either light or dark, a medium-tone carpet will hide the most dirt marks. Carpeting that has a blend of colors or a pattern hides dirt better than solid-color carpets do. Carpet should not be used in entry areas, such as vestibules, which are subject to heavy, continual dirt accumulation. Ceramic tile, or some other easy-to-clean material, is a better choice for entry areas. Similarly, other high-traffic areas, such as cash counters, may require hard or resilient flooring materials rather than carpeting.

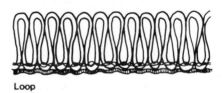

Loop

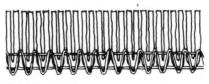

Cut-pile

5-1. Two major styles of carpet are available, loop and cut pile.

Resilient Floors
Asphalt, Vinyl, and Rubber Tile. Resilient floors, as the name suggests, permit surface deflection and spring back from impact or loading. Resilient tile is not commonly used in the sales areas of most retail stores, but is frequently used in storage and other back rooms. Most shopping-center landlords will not permit the less expensive resilient floors, such as asphalt or vinyl-composition tiles, in sales areas, although other resilient materials such as rubber sheet flooring, are increasingly being accepted for such use.

Asphalt tiles are suitable for storage areas and are the least expensive type of resilient flooring. However, they are less flexible and stain resistant than are other tiles, and are available only in marbleized finish—good reasons to limit their use to areas not seen by customers. Vinyl-composition tiles are also commonly used in the back areas of retail stores. They are superior in grease and stain resistance, durability, and ease of maintenance. Vinyl-composition tiles contain limestone fillers, and are different from pure vinyl tiles, discussed below. Rubber tiles are less grease resistant than vinyl-composition tiles are, but offer excellent resilience, sound absorption, and stain resistance. These tiles are more expensive than the vinyl-composition or asphalt tile.

Vinyl tiles offer pure, homogeneous color and excellent performance. They are denser, less porous, more flexible, and up to four or five times as expensive than vinyl-composition tiles. While more expensive than asphalt, vinyl-composition, or rubber tiles, vinyl tiles are an acceptable, cost-saving alternative to ceramic tile where appearance is important.

Raised rubber or vinyl tiles or sheets are gaining acceptance as sales-area materials. They are relatively expensive and have the same characteristics as rubber or vinyl tiles except for the raised circular, square, or rectangular surface patterns. The materials are very durable and have been used successfully in such high-traffic locations as airport terminals.

Wood Floors. Wood floors are a possible alternative to carpeted floors. They offer the warmth and richness of the natural material, excellent durability, and reasonable cost (including installation charges, the least expensive wood floor costs about the same as the most expensive commercial carpeting). Unlike carpeting, they do not offer acoustical absorption, but the sound of feet on a wood floor often creates a sense of action and excitement within a store and may, for that reason, be highly appropriate for a store that sells toys or sporting goods. They are considered resilient, and so are more comfortable underfoot than ceramic tile or other nonresilient materials.

Wood floors are composed of wood strips, planks, or parquet tiles. Depending on which type is used, wood floors may be glued to a concrete floor or nailed to a wooden subfloor. The subfloor may have a subgrid of wooden sleepers—members nailed to the subfloor at 12-inch intervals to level the subfloor. In general, storeowners choose strips, planks, or parquet tiles made of oak or maple, which are relatively inexpensive; the more durable teak and walnut are probably too expensive for most stores.

Wood strips 1½ to 2¼ inches wide and of varying lengths are laid adjacent to one another to form parallel, basketweave, herringbone, or other patterns perpendicular or at a forty-five-degree angle to the wall. Strip flooring usually must be installed over a subgrid of wooden sleepers. Planks are wider (3¼ inches or more) and usually thinner than strips, whereas parquet tiles are available in 9-inch to 19-inch squares and have a decorative geometric pattern. If the retail store is located in a shopping center that has a concrete floor, the only practical flooring solution may be to install a plank or parquet wood floor. In this case, parquet tiles or planks ⅜ to ½ inch thick are glued to the concrete. If the existing floor has a noticeable depression, a skim coat of cement should be applied to level the concrete floor before the wood is installed.

Wood floors may be purchased prefinished or unfinished. After they are installed, unfinished floors are sanded smooth, sealed with a penetrating sealer to prevent staining, and then finished. If finished with wax, the floor may later be repaired if damaged without refinishing the floor. If the floor is finished with varnish or polyurethane these finishes must be sanded down and refinished if the floor is damaged. Moisture-curing polyurethane is usually specified for high-traffic floors because of its hard finish.

Nonresilient Floors

Ceramic Tile. Paving tiles are a modular ceramic flooring material and have a fascial area exceeding 6 square inches. They are usually available in square, rectangular, or hexagonal shapes. Relatively thin in relation to their face area, paving tiles are made from baked uniform-composition clay or a mixture of clay and other ceramic materials and are available in a glazed or unglazed finish. Glazed tile has a fused impervious facial finish that is categorized by the nature of its water-absorption qualities, which ranges from nonvitreous (more than 7 percent water absorption) to impervious (less than .5 percent water absorption). Since the glaze is applied to the surface after the tiles are baked, glazed tiles are available in many different colors. Although the glazing is subject to wear, many glazed tile types are guaranteed to last beyond the average lease term. The durability of the glaze is expressed in a rating that ranges from 1 to 4, with 4 being the surface most resistant to wear.

Unglazed tile derives its color from the material of which it is made. The color and surface of unglazed tile is uniform and, because these tiles have no wearing surface to break down, they are extremely durable. They are available in the same range of water absorption as glazed tiles. Unglazed quarry tiles are floor paving tiles composed of natural, earth-tone clays. They are susceptible to grease staining, however, and should be sealed with wax, tile sealer, or oil-based cleaning agents before first use.

Both glazed and unglazed ceramic tile may be impregnated with an abrasive surface aggregate of silicon carbide or similar rustproof abrasive to make the tiles slip-resistant. This abrasive should be used if any water is likely to be present in the tiled area, since wet tiles are slippery. Tiles usually are available in such trim units (or edge shapes) as cove base (a right-angle corner shape) or bullnose (a rounded edge), but not all tiles are available with all trim units. If special trim units are required, the designer should determine whether they are available in the tile desired.

Ceramic tile may be installed thin-set in a thin coat of organic adhesive, cement, or epoxy. The subfloor should first be cleaned of all foreign materials, for if this is not done, tiles may dislodge. Then, the tile setter will trowel on a thin layer of cement or adhesive and set the tile in this adhesive with a light tamp. After the tiles have been laid, the floor should set for a day, after which the joints between tiles are grouted. The thin-setting method of installation is used most commonly in store areas not requiring special floor drainage. If it is necessary to slope the floor to a drain, the mud-set method of installation may be used. In this method, the tile is thin-set on a previously laid bed of cement mortar at least 1¼ inches thick. This cement mortar is sloped to provide proper drainage, as for a kitchen or bathroom floor.

Masonry. The use of stone or masonry floors in retail stores is limited. Although these materials will clearly outlast the term of most leases, they are expensive and in most cases must be installed in floor depressions. However, both granite and marble are available in ⅜-inch-thick tiles which may be thin-set. If the floor is likely to get wet occasionally, such as in a vestibule, a rough finish may be used to increase safety. Another drawback to using polished granite or marble is that they can be scratched by foot traffic. Slate is a less-expensive, naturally rough stone floor that provides a quality image and durable surface (fig. 5-2).

Terrazzo. Terrazzo is a mixture of stone chips (commonly marble or, less often, granite) in a cement or resinous matrix, which is divided into sections, ground, and polished. It is a very durable, low-maintenance flooring material that can be thin-set. The stone chips, matrix, and dividing strips are available in many different colors, permitting a variety of possible designs. Its cost is in the range of the more expensive ceramic tiles, and like ceramic tile it offers a hard, durable, walking surface (fig. 5-3).

Walls. The typical interior wall for retail stores in shopping centers is constructed of metal studs with a gypsum board (drywall) finish (fig. 5-4). The metal studs are nonbearing, roll-formed, vertical sheet metal framing members spaced 16 to 24 inches on center with a width ranging from 1⅝ to 6 inches. Their surface has a regular pattern of slots, which permits pipes, cables, or conduits to run concealed within the wall. The studs are set in top and bottom metal runners and screwed into place. Gypsum board, typically ⅝ of an inch thick for retail construction, is then screwed to the studs in panels that are 4 feet high and 8 to 14 feet wide. The joints between the panels and the recessed screw heads are covered with joint compound and tape, then sanded to achieve a smooth finished wall surface, which may be fire-rated and water resistant, depending on the type of gypsum board used. Metal studs have virtually replaced wood studs in retail construction. Commonly, the landlord in a shopping center will provide the studs and, in some cases, gypsum board finish for the demising wall, with the remainder of the walls to be completed by the tenant. Gypsum board for the demising wall runs from the floor to the underside of the structural deck above to provide a fire-rated wall.

Frequently, service corridor walls are constructed by the landlord of concrete masonry units (CMUs) and these walls also serve as the tenant's demising

5-2. Slate floors are durable and offer an interesting rough texture.
(Photography: Karant & Associates, Inc.)

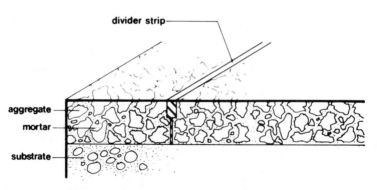

5-3. Section of a terrazzo floor.

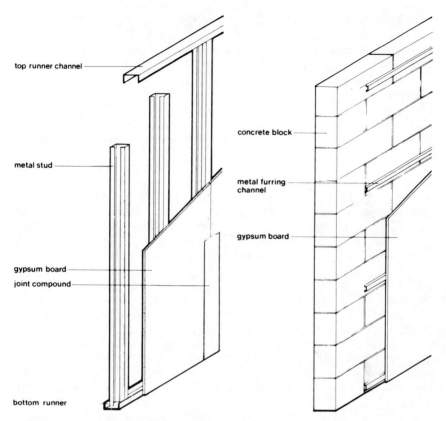

top runner channel

concrete block

metal stud

metal furring channel

gypsum board

gypsum board

joint compound

bottom runner

5-4 and 5-5. A masonry wall with metal furring and gypsum board.

walls. The tenant will then either leave the masonry wall unfinished, if it is in a storage space, or add metal furring strips ⅞ inch deep, to which ⅝ inch drywall is attached and finished (fig. 5-5).

Interior walls may run from the floor to the bottom of a suspended ceiling or through the ceiling to the structure above. Often, the gypsum is stopped about 6 inches above the ceiling. This method is more economical, and permits the area above the ceiling to function as a return air plenum for ventilation. The gypsum board of interior walls may be extended to the structural deck above for sound-absorption or fire-rating purposes. If the shopping-center landlord requires the tenant's space to be sound isolated—if, for example, the tenant runs a games arcade or a music store—sound batts should be placed between the metal studs.

Interior walls may also be less than full height, serving as partial screens. Walls of partial height may be constructed of metal studs and gypsum board, but they must be reinforced inside the wall with additional structural members such as steel pipes and flanges that are connected to the floor and that brace the top of the wall. The wall may also be braced from its top to a structural element above the ceiling. The tenant can choose to finish interior and demising walls with a variety of finishes or leave them unfinished if equipment or cabinetry is to be placed next to the wall.

Plaster

Plaster, used as a veneer or in place of gypsum board, offers a variety of textures and may be formed to almost any shape, permitting curved walls or soffits. Gypsum board cannot be used to form curved wall corners of very tight radii (under 18 inches); plaster is generally used instead. Plaster walls may be constructed using a combination of metal lath and coats of plaster, or may be made with a base layer of special gypsum board finished with a coat of plaster. If tight curves or other special shapes are required, the metal lath and plaster process must be used to achieve the desired shape. Plaster finishes may be trowelled or sprayed on to form surfaces ranging from smooth to very rough stucco; the surface is usually then finished with paint. Plaster is more durable than gypsum board and may be used in public areas within the store.

Paint

The most common and least expensive finish for walls is paint. Paint is available in three basic finishes: gloss, semigloss, and flat. Heavy textured paints that simulate the look of stucco or sand plaster are also available. Both water-based and solvent-based paints are used in retail stores. Typically, a prime coating and one or two finish coats are applied to the raw walls. Painting is a simple way to color and finish a wall surface, and it will protect the surface from dirt and moisture. However, paint does not protect a surface from the effects of impact or continual wear, so paint should usually be confined to areas not touched by the public, such as ceilings and the walls of storage rooms, offices, or areas behind displays. Of course, the store's budget may dictate painting walls in areas of heavy use, but more durable finish materials should be used if possible. If surfaces are to be painted, gloss or semigloss paint should be used on doors, trim, and other high-contact areas; flat paint may be used on walls.

Wallcoverings

Wallcoverings are flexible sheet materials applied to walls with adhesive and include wallpaper, fabric, and vinyl. Wallpaper is available in rolls 27 to 54 inches wide and comes in a myriad of colors and patterns. Wallpaper is more varied than paint in the areas of color and pattern, but it offers little more protection than paint does from wear and tear. In fact, it is frequently more difficult to clean fingerprints from wallpaper than paint, unless the wallpaper is a cleanable type. For this reason, wallpaper should generally be used only on out-of-reach walls.

Fabric wallcoverings such as burlap may be more durable than paint or wallpaper but are very difficult to clean. In addition, fabric must be treated chemically to bring it up to the fire safety standards of most local building codes. This procedure can add a week or two to the construction schedule of the store, however, while the fabric is sent out to be chemically treated. Fabrics are appropriate for display-window backgrounds or other areas not touched by the public. Certain ribbed fabrics are moderately sound absorbing and hide flaws on the walls underneath; screws and nails can be attached or removed and the fabric will hide the damaged surface underneath. Velcro fasteners can also be attached to ribbed material and used to hang light-weight products. Ribbed fabric is very useful for art galleries or other stores that often hang products on their walls.

Vinyl wallcovering is usually available in 54-inch widths and offers a wide selection of colors, finishes, and thicknesses. Since vinyl is a plastic material, many surface textures are possible. Some textures are imitations of burlap, linen, or other fabrics, some of leather, and others of wood: of the imitations, the most successful are the leather-look, suede, and pigskin varieties. Vinyls are also available in plain finishes, or with ribs or other raised geometric patterns. Vinyl is the most durable and easy to clean of the three wallcoverings, and is suitable for most interior walls. It does not easily stain, rip, tear, or dent. Properly installed, it provides a nearly seamless, uniform, cleanable surface. Vinyl wall-covering has been extensively tested by manufacturers to determine flame spread and the smoke it contributes in fires. The test results for each wallcovering type are stated in the manufacturers' catalogs. Therefore, satisfying local fire-safety codes is simply a matter of selecting the vinyl with the correct test results. Unlike fabrics, no further treatment is necessary.

Wood

Wood wall finishings consist of panels or boards of varying quality, ranging from finished hardwood to rough-sawn softwood. Panels are usually several feet wide, whereas boards are limited in width to about 12 inches. Softwoods include pine, birch, cedar, and redwood. Hardwoods include walnut, rose-wood, mahogany, ash, oak, and teak. Oak, red or white, is used most often in retail stores because it is cost-effective. Teak and mahogany are more ex-pensive, but may be within the storeowner's budget.

Veneer plywood is often used as wood paneling. A surface layer of finish hardwood veneer is laminated to a base wood to form a ¾-inch-thick material. Hardwood veneer is available in many different species and several different veneer cuts. Each cutting method produces a different grain appearance so that the same tree will produce substantially different veneers, depending on how it is cut. The five cutting methods are rotary, rift, plain slicing, quarter slicing, and half-round slicing (fig. 5-6). Rotary cutting is the least expensive method and produces a very bold random grain that is difficult to match at joints. Plain, quarter, and rift-cut slicing produce more uniform, tight, and vertical-patterned grains. Half-round slicing shows the graining characteristics of both rotary and plain slicing. The designer should review samples of each available cut for the wood species selected to ascertain the desired look.

Hardwood paneling is available in premium, custom, and economy grades. Grading refers to the absence or presence of defects in the veneer face; pre-mium-grade veneer has the fewest defects and costs substantially more than custom grade. In most cases, the budget of a retail store will dictate using

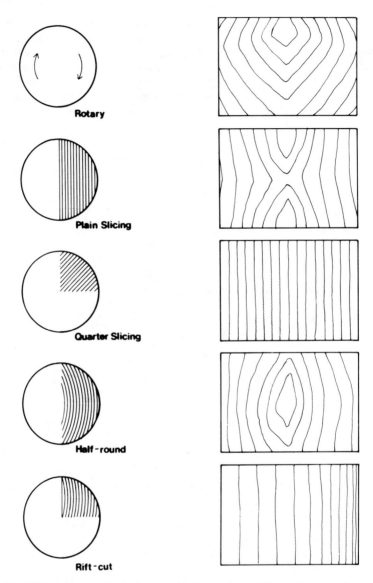

5-6. The different wood-cutting methods produce different types of veneers.

custom-grade paneling. Paneling that is plain-sliced, rift-cut, or quarter-sliced may be installed in a matching pattern, such as book match, slip match, or random match (fig. 5-7). In book matching, each veneer piece is joined to connect the grains. Slip matching places veneers in the order in which they were cut from the log, but does not match or join the grain. Random matching makes no attempt to match veneers at the grain. When matched premium-

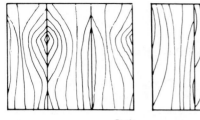 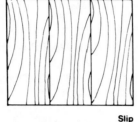 

Book   **Slip**   **Random**

5-7. Different patterns of veneer matching may be used for paneled walls.

grade panels are used, the panels can be detailed flush to deemphasize joints. In a less expensive installation method, veneers would not be matched; solid battens might be placed at the joint between panels to separate the visual change from one panel to another.

Solid hardwood is also available in premium, custom, and economy grades. If the wood is exposed and a transparent finish is to be used, premium-grade solid pieces should be selected. If the hardwood will be painted with an opaque finish, custom-grade wood may be used. Solid hardwood panels are extremely expensive and are not normally used in retail stores, although solid hardwood can be used for moldings if the wood will be physically exposed to the public. One-inch squares or other shapes of hardwood may be used to form parallel vertical battens that alternatively expose and cover the base finish material underneath—the plaster, paint, or wallcovering. This is an interesting but expensive wall treatment and should be used sparingly or where budget permits.

Softwoods, like hardwoods, may be milled to all the traditional molding shapes—crown, quarter-round, half-round, and so on. Or, the designer may custom design a molding shape for the store, which adds the cost of the cutting knives to the other costs, but otherwise is not unduly expensive. Solid-board softwoods, such as cedar, may be used to provide the richness and warmth of real wood paneling at an affordable cost.

Wood wall installations may be painted or stained to bring out the grain or simulate more expensive wood, then sealed with lacquer, varnish, vinyl, oil, or synthetic enamel. Each finish has its own performance and appearance properties; care should be taken in selecting a finish that will achieve the desired effect. Lacquer, it should be noted, increases the flame spread of wood, and may be undesirable for that reason.

Many shopping-center landlords and code authorities will require wood to be treated to reduce the flame spread of the material. Some fire-safety codes allow the use of fire retardant that is painted directly on the wood. This method may be used, where permitted, for concealed wood only, as the fire retardant ruins the wood finish. The other method involves impregnating the wood with pressure-treated mineral salts—an expensive procedure that must be conducted off-site, at a treatment plant. Some fire-retardant methods affect the wood so that it cannot be milled after treatment. Because fire-retardant treatment will affect the way the wood takes a stain or finish, samples of the wood should be fire-treated, stained, and finished for the designer's approval before the wood is ordered.

Hardboard, Metal, and Plastic Wall Paneling

Wall paneling may be purchased as stock or custom fabricated. Stock paneling for retail-store use includes many variations of hardboard and formed sheet metals. Hardboard paneling is a ¼ inch thick, wood-composition material that simulates solid wood paneling and is an inexpensive alternative to other materials. Hardboard is thinner and more brittle than particleboard, and is used more as paneling than for cabinet construction. Hardboard is also available in laminated wood veneers, called tambour, that have been scored to create a wood batten effect. Tambour is flexible in one direction and can be bent around curved walls or columns (fig. 5-8). Metal panels of sheet-formed stainless steel in anodized aluminum finishes are available with many different embossed geometric patterns. They offer an interesting but expensive alternative to typical wall finishing materials.

Paneling may also be custom designed and fabricated for an individual retail store. Plastic or metal laminated panels are commonly used. These are made from ¾ inch particleboard with a layer of plastic or metal approximately ¹⁄₁₆ inch thick laminated to its surface. Plastic laminates are available in many different colors, finishes, and patterns. They are very durable, resist impact, and

5-8. Flexible wood veneer hardboard that has been scored to give a wood batten effect.

are easy to clean, but are susceptible to chipping at corners. New types of solid-color plastic laminates are now available that provide color throughout the material, which effectively eliminates the dark edge typically formed where laminates meet at a corner. Through-color laminates may also have patterns routed out of or sandblasted into them, creating many possibilities for mural designs. Metal laminates are available in all different metal types and finishes, including aluminum, stainless steel, copper, and brass. When laminated to particleboard, they form a very durable, distinctive surface. Other kinds of panels may be created as well, in compositions of particleboard and other materials: acoustical sheet material, for example, may be laminated to particleboard and fabric stretched overall to form an attractive, sound-absorbent, tackable surface. Custom panels are typically hung on wall cleats which form a dovetailed, gravity-supported connection between the panel and the wall (fig. 5-9). When this type of installation is used, the panel can be removed and replaced later if necessary.

Mirrors and Other Glass
Mirrors as a wall finishing material must be carefully considered in the design. Typically, mirrors are used to create the illusion of more space. However, this desirable effect is sometimes outweighed by the confusing effect the mirror may have on the shopper. Or, mirrors may reflect undesirable images, such as other storefronts and signs, light sources, back rooms, and so on. Mirrors for commercial installation are ¼ inch thick, glued to the wall, and held in place with small channels at top and bottom. They are available in clear, gray, and bronze finishes and their edges should be ground smooth (designer should specify this when ordering).

Glass may also be back painted (which provides an interesting, smooth, and colorful look), sandblasted, or acid-etched. Painted glass is mounted as

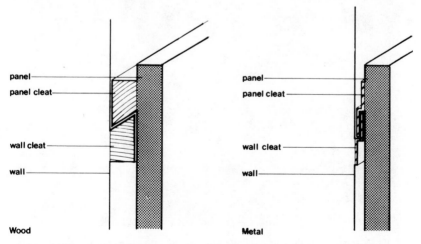

panel
panel cleat

wall cleat
wall

Wood

panel
panel cleat

wall cleat
wall

Metal

5-9. Two common methods for the support of wall panels.

mirrors are, but care must be taken to ensure that the glass will not pull away from the wall, or its paint may chip off. The wall should be smooth, to prevent areas of uneven stress on the glass, and the glass should be set in top and bottom metal channels. Etched or sandblasted glass are two relatively inexpensive ways to introduce ornamental elements into the decor. Clear, etched, or painted glass may be framed to create a partition, but this glass should be safety protected—tempered, laminated, or embedded with wire—to prevent shattering if the glass is broken.

Glass is difficult to work with as paneling. The design of a glass-panel wall should be simple and unbroken; if glass must be cut out for outlets or switches or if L-shaped patterns are used, the glass will weaken and probably break upon installation. Glass blocks—thick masonry units that are laid like concrete blocks—can be used to form partitions, low walls, or as wall surfaces, but are very expensive.

Tile and Masonry Finishes

Ceramic tiles used as wall finishes are available in a wide variety of shapes, sizes, and colors. They provide a durable, interesting, but expensive wall surface. Ceramic tiles may be custom designed and manufactured to create interesting and durable wall murals (fig. 5-10). Thin (½ inch) brick-shape tiles may be used to simulate a brick wall. Walls of marble or granite, except in tile form, are usually not used in retail stores because of their prohibitive cost.

5-10. A custom-designed ceramic tile mural. *(Photography: Barry Rustin)*

CEILINGS

Retail store ceilings serve many purposes. They serve as a finished overhead horizontal surface; they conceal electrical, plumbing, and HVAC equipment; they may provide acoustical control; they may provide an illuminated surface for indirect light fixtures; they may create a plenum space that is used as a return air duct; and they may provide the required fire-resistant material separating the space below from the structural steel decking and framing above. Ceilings in retail stores should be relatively neutral in design. While ceilings may have pattern, it is best if it is simple and repetitive; and while color may be desirable, only one color should be used. This downplaying of what is typically a significant architectural element in other buildings is suggested because unusual ceilings draw the customer's eye to the ceiling and away from the merchandise. Unless the merchandise is common and the space ambiance more important than a view of the product, ceilings should be simple, unobtrusive planes.

Store ceilings are typically suspended (below all the mechanical and electrical equipment they conceal) by a structural metal grid connected above by wires to the building structure. For maintenance purposes, ceilings must provide access to all piping and equipment; the ceiling must either be fully accessible or have service access panels, large enough to accommodate a person's shoulders, placed in appropriate locations, such as below plumbing cleanouts (access points) and near blowers, heating coils, and other equipment.

Ceilings can be modified to change the proportions of a room. By raising the ceiling, one can create a room of expanded proportions that can accommodate larger-scale items such as furniture. By lowering the ceiling, a more intimate room can be created, to focus attention on smaller products, such as shoes or accessories. Partial ceilings or soffits are often used for this purpose. Placing soffits above wall displays permits the integration of continuous lighting and focuses attention on the wall-displayed product, while the center areas of the room may have a higher ceiling more appropriate to the scale of merchandise displayed there.

Where a ceiling is not required for fire-protection purposes, the designer may choose not to construct a dropped ceiling. The space above and all the equipment therein could be painted a single dark color, with the lighting fixtures dropped to a point below all equipment and piping. The dark color could be extended to the bottom of the light fixtures and serve as a ceiling demarcation, drawing the eye of the customer only as far as the line of the light fixtures, bright against the dark ceiling. It is usually not good practice to paint an exposed ceiling a light color, as this will attract the customer's eyes to the ceiling and away from the merchandise. An exception to this rule occurs if the store's product or concept is a playful one, such as children's toys. Then, piping and ductwork could be painted bright colors against the white background of an exposed ceiling for an interesting and appropriate effect. Eliminating the suspended ceiling creates an additional problem, however; its removal means there is no barrier between the dust, scaling, moisture, and other debris that may fall from the equipment, roof, or floor above.

A well-designed ceiling integrates all elements—lights, diffusers, returns, and sprinkler heads—carefully. This is most important in ceilings with a strong grid pattern. While few shoppers will take note of a well-designed ceiling, they will subconsciously notice one that is poorly designed. Their attention may be drawn to sprinkler heads placed too close to diffusers or located off the overall ceiling grid The design of the ceiling, which includes the layout of all its lighting and mechanical elements, should be integrated with the displays, walls, and floor patterns below to create a single, unified design.

Acoustic Ceilings

Acoustic ceilings are the most frequently installed ceilings in retail stores. They are composed of a metal grid framework that is suspended from the above structure by wires and completed with modular tiles or panels. Acoustic ceilings require no additional finishing and provide good sound control. Their removable panels offer easy access to the mechanical and electrical systems that they conceal. Some types also provide fire protection for the structural elements above. A wide variety of building components have been designed to integrate with the grid system of acoustic ceilings, including fluorescent light fixtures, HVAC diffusers and returns, and communications systems. In fact, this ceiling has become an entire construction system, with many different parties participating in the manufacture of its many components. It is relatively inexpensive, considering its many features, and has become quite popular.

Acoustic tiles or panels are manufactured from mineral fibers bonded by organic and inorganic materials and cast on trays for heat curing. They are available in a variety of surface textures and grid patterns, such as colored, wood-look, mirrored, and simulated pressed-metal patterned tiles. Tiles are

5-11. Scored acoustic-tile ceiling panels produce a neutral, geometric grid. *(Courtesy of Armstrong Commercial Ceilings)*

available in 12 × 12, 12 × 24, 24 × 24, and 24 × 48 inch sizes. Using the larger panel sizes is more economical, since fewer suspension and grid members are required. The large panels are available in a scored grid to make them appear as smaller tiles (fig. 5-11).

Acoustic ceilings provide excellent noise control and are available with NRC ratings of .50 to .85, depending on the style of tile used. NRC (noise reduction coefficient) is a measure of sound absorbed by a material. The higher the rating, the greater the sound control. Acoustic tiles have a porous composition that controls sound energy and dissipates it internally, so that sound is not reflected to the environment below.

Another major advantage of an accoustical tile ceiling is the fire-protection properties that most acoustic tiles can provide. They are noncombustible and may be fire rated, providing one to four hours of fire protection depending on the type of tile, suspension system, and the floor or roof construction above. When used as a fire-rated system, acoustic ceilings must have special tiles, suspension grid, and grid components. The ceiling system should be specified to meet the desired rating.

Two basic types of acoustic tile suspension systems are available: exposed grid and concealed spline systems. Exposed grid systems are composed of grid elements that are **T** shaped in sections (fig. 5-12). The **T** is inverted so

5-12. A recessed acoustic-tile ceiling with a larger grid pattern. *(Courtesy of Armstrong Commercial Ceilings)*

that the bottom legs of the **T** support the tile at its four edges. While this grid is always exposed to view, it may be recessed ⅜ inch from the surface of the tile, or the bottom legs of the **T** may form a channel from which elements below may be suspended or attached (fig. 5-13). The suspension grid may be painted the same color as the ceiling tiles or a contrasting color.

Concealed spline suspension systems for acoustic ceilings are not visible when completed. This results in a single surface that aesthetically is an alternative to gypsum board but that has other properties as well, such as sound control. Concealed splines are **C**- or **Z**-shaped suspension members designed to work with 12 × 12 or 12 × 24 inch tiles. The tile is slotted to slide into the spline and conceal it. Concealed spline ceilings are more expensive than exposed grid systems and are not easily accessible unless matching access panels are specified; otherwise, the interlocking tiles must all be removed to gain access.

Gypsum Board and Plaster Ceilings

Gypsum board ceilings provide a smooth, continuous ceiling plane that may be painted any color. While they do not offer the acoustical properties of acoustical tile ceilings, they are exceptionally good as light reflectors for indirect lighting systems. However, unless an exceptionally noisy selling environment is desired, a gypsum board ceiling should not be used in a space with hard-surface flooring. If the floor is carpeted, however, noise should not be a problem. Gypsum board also may be used as a border material for an exposed-grid, acoustic tile ceiling to create a more expensive-looking finished product. Since exposed grid acoustic tile is on a 2 × 2-foot grid and since many shopping centers have 25 × 25-foot structural bay systems, integrating the exposed ceiling grid with the building columns will result in partial and **L**-shaped tiles at the columns. This can be avoided by creating a major grid pattern of approximately 3-foot-wide gypsum board bands on column center lines, which eliminates the difficult intersection of acoustical tile at columns and creates bays of whole acoustic tiles between columns (fig. 5-14). The gypsum board may be screwed directly into the suspension system of the acoustical ceiling and edged with **J**-shaped molding. Gypsum board may also be used as a

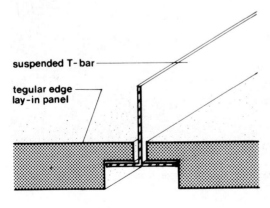

suspended T-bar

tegular edge
lay-in panel

5-13. Section of a recessed-grid acoustic ceiling.

soffit material in conjunction with acoustical tile anywhere an accent is desirable, such as a feature display area. Mixing the materials permits a blend of the beneficial properties of both materials in one ceiling. Gypsum board provides fire protection as a ceiling material, but the combination of gypsum board and the particular structure above may not have received an official UL rating. If a fire rating is required, this factor should be addressed with the building department authorities.

Plaster ceilings are rarely used in retail stores because they are expensive and their installation is time-consuming. However, if a special ceiling is required, such as a dome or a vault, plaster may be the best material to use. Also, if this special ceiling area is to be uplighted, plaster provides a very smooth, regular surface not attainable with gypsum board. Plaster, like gypsum board, is a sound reflector and this must be considered in a design. Plaster can also be used as a special veneer finish and is an inexpensive way to achieve a stucco or sand-plaster look.

Aluminum Ceilings

Aluminum ceilings are available in many forms: in square panels that lie in exposed supporting grids or slide into concealed grids; in slats; or in coffered grids. Aluminum ceilings may be solid or perforated in a tight, uniform pattern of small holes. If the aluminum is perforated, a layer of sound batting may be placed above the panel or slats to provide good acoustical control; nonperforated aluminum ceilings tend, on the other hand, to be noisy. Available in many different finishes and colors, aluminum provides an exciting alternative to acoustical tile. However, if a fire-rated ceiling is required, a gypsum board or a fire-rated acoustical ceiling must be placed above the aluminum ceiling. Aluminum ceilings are three to four times as expensive as acoustic tile or gypsum board ceilings. The square-panel exposed- or concealed-grid aluminum

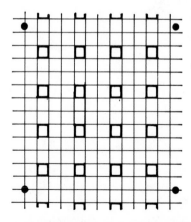 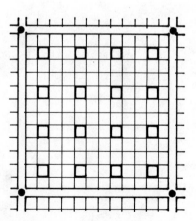

5-14. A major grid consisting of bands of gypsum board may be used to solve the problem of integrating 2-foot acoustic tiles into a standard 25-foot-square structural bay system.

5-15. A slat aluminum ceiling system. *(Photography: Barry Rustin)*

5-16. A coffered open-cell aluminum ceiling system. *(Ceiling system: Magnagrid by Intalite; photography: Idaka)*

ceiling is similar in construction to and has the same accessibility as a typical acoustic tile ceiling.

The slat aluminum ceiling is composed of a suspended metal grid to which are attached aluminum slats formed into channels approximately 3¼ to 4 inches wide and ⅝ inch deep, separated by ½-inch gaps (fig. 5-15). A system of light fixtures and HVAC diffusers is now available that can be integrated with the ceiling materials. The slats can be oriented to parallel walls or run on a 45-degree or other angle. This is a very interesting and uniform ceiling.

Open-cell or *coffered* aluminum ceilings consist of rectangular, formed aluminum sections assembled to create an open grid of uniform, square cells 3 to 6 inches wide. Overall, the ceiling forms an eggcrate pattern (fig. 5-16). The aluminum sections may be from 1 to 4 inches deep. Since it is an open grid, sprinkler heads and exhaust or supply diffusers can be hidden above the ceiling grid; light fixtures can fit into larger cells or hang through the grid. Usually, the entire area above the ceiling is painted a dark color to reduce visibility through the grid to the mechanical and electrical systems above. One dis-

5-17. A luminous fabric ceiling combines a colorful, sculptural effect with general lighting. (Design: LUBOTSKY, METTER, WORTHINGTON + LAW, LTD.; photography: Karant & Associates, Inc.)

advantage is that this ceiling offers no protection from fire. Although it is expensive, the coffered aluminum grid ceiling does have the advantage, however, of hiding many elements, such as sprinkler heads and diffusers, above the ceiling surface—it is an interesting, uncluttered, and neutral ceiling that should enhance the merchandise of almost any retail store.

Special Ceilings

Mirrored ceilings can be made of polished aluminum tiles set in a grid or of plastic mirrors laminated with adhesive to gypsum board and secured with mechanical fasteners. However, using genuine glass mirrors overhead is not recommended, even if safety glass is used, because of the difficulty and expense of supporting the relatively heavy material properly.

Wood ceiling grids, lattices, beams, and coffers may be custom built or purchased as stock items and used to construct ceilings. Wood, however, even if fire-treated, may be prohibited as a ceiling material by local fire codes. To solve the fire-code problem, synthetic, incombustible, fiberform-reinforced gypsum panels that rest in an exposed grid may be used. These are designed to have the look of a classic, coffered, carved wood ceiling, and provide full access to the plenum above.

Plastic ceiling materials simulating stained glass are available. Plastic "stained glass" ceilings are a dubious choice for most retail stores, however, and may also be prohibited by fire codes.

Fabric ceilings are often distinctive and colorful, as shown in figure 5-17, but they must, of course, be made of fire-treated material. Typically the fabric is hung vertically in a geometric pattern; fluorescent lighting can be placed above the ceiling for a luminous effect. This ceiling conceals all diffusers, registers, sprinkler heads, and lights while providing good acoustical control.

SIX

LIGHTING

Lighting is the single most important factor in the design of a retail store. Good lighting can enhance a product's appearance, accentuate a special display, balance the visual elements of a store, and create the proper mood. The first objective of store lighting is to establish the store image. Lighting is a central design element that, in combination with the other design elements of the store, conveys to the shopper the value of the products sold. If the store lighting imparts a look of importance to the product, it will appear valuable; if the lighting imparts a look of commonness to the product, it will seem less valuable. Even if the merchandise is exactly the same in each store, it will be perceived as having different values. Discount stores are illuminated with harsh, diffuse, overhead lighting, quality stores with glare-free, directional, display illumination. It is important to recognize that the store's image can be established by its lighting. Is price the most important factor? Then the lighting must make the merchandise look common. Are quality, uniqueness, and style the most important factors? Then the lighting must focus on the merchandise and make it look special. If properly designed, lighting can give the shopper a reason to enter or to pass the store, depending on his shopping goals. Budget-minded shoppers, it is important to note, will pass by a store that looks "too expensive" even if the merchandise is reasonably priced. Store image must be presented correctly to satisfy customer expectations.

The second objective of lighting is to attract the shopper to the store; to focus the customer's interest on this one store as he walks along a street or mall of many stores. Well-designed lighting can attract potential customers as successfully as a sale sign can. Lighting can also attract the customer to a certain display, or draw him toward the interior of the store, thereby increasing the possibility of purchase.

The third objective of good store lighting is to provide the right sales environment for the product. To display the merchandise properly, lighting must attract shoppers and enhance the quality of the product, presenting its detail, material, and color in the best light. If the product is removed from the display for inspection by the customer, lighting must permit him to evaluate the product or enable the salesperson to explain its features. Often products look excellent under display lighting, but appear less desirable if removed from that light. Lighting must be designed to increase sales.

The last objective of lighting is to facilitate the closing of the sale. Sales and stock areas must be well lit so that salespersons can complete the sales transaction and deliver the product.

The process of designing lighting for retail stores has three elements: identifying the task areas of the store to be illuminated; reviewing and determining lighting criteria appropriate to each task area; and selecting light sources that will satisfy the lighting criteria (fig. 6-1).

LIGHTING TASK AREAS

Within any retail store, the functional operations to be illuminated can be divided into three lighting task areas—display, product evaluation, and service areas. The lighting requirements of each area are usually very different.

After the preliminary floor plan has been developed and all the basic elements of the store design determined, the designer should review the plan and identify each area in terms of lighting function (fig. 6-2). It should be noted that there often will be an overlap of lighting task areas; that is, the same floor area may be used for display, product evaluation, and service. However, lighting must be precisely designed to accommodate each movement of the product. A product on a display shelf attracts the customer, who may first gaze at it to evaluate its shape and form, remove it for closer evaluation, and then hand it to the clerk for wrapping and purchase. The shelf, the customer's hands, and the clerk's service area—each part of the sequence described above—must be properly analyzed and illuminated. Aisles or corridors, unless isolated or very wide, are not usually specifically illuminated, but rely on wash light— light spilling over from other areas.

Display Areas

Display areas make the product visible to the customer. Some display areas feature products selected by the storeowner for special attention such as a show-window display of mannequins. These areas are generally more isolated, inaccessible, and highly illuminated than other display areas. The primary purpose of feature displays is to attract customer attention and interest to an individual product or special group of products. The primary purpose of merchandising displays—the other type of display area—is to attract the customer's attention and interest to an array of products. The products in mer-

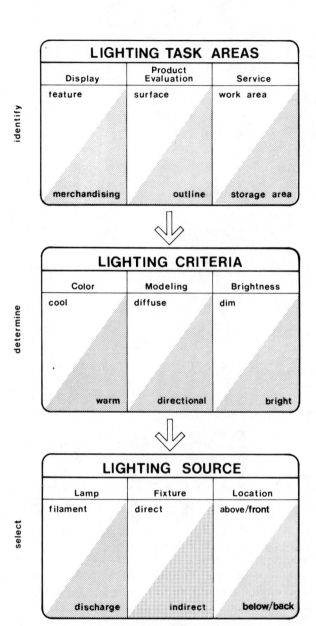

6-1. The three elements of lighting design.

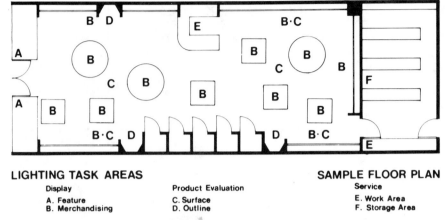

LIGHTING TASK AREAS

Display	Product Evaluation	SAMPLE FLOOR PLAN Service
A. Feature	C. Surface	E. Work Area
B. Merchandising	D. Outline	F. Storage Area

6-2. The different lighting task areas are identified by function on the preliminary floor plan.

chandise displays are usually open to inspection, such as on open tables or shelving, and can be handled.

Product Evaluation Areas

After a customer has become interested in a product, he will then evaluate it. This task area (product evaluation) has two subcategory possibilities that depend on the nature of the visual task: evaluations that concern the surface of a product, and evaluations that concern the outline of a product. Both types of evaluation may be required before the customer decides to buy the product, and the evaluations may take place in two locations. For instance, an opaque vase could be displayed on a frosted glass shelf, illuminated from below against a contrasting background to present the vase's outline, proportions, and specular qualities. However, the surface detail may not be clear, in which case the customer will remove the vase from the shelf to view its surface detail and color. Another light source, which will permit accurate rendering of all surface details and color, will be required for this surface evaluation.

Clothing is often displayed on mannequins to present an overall effect and emphasize both outline and surface detail. Clothing that is merchandised on racks will usually be picked up by the customer for evaluation. At this phase— either looking at a mannequin or examining clothing taken from a rack—the customer is interested in style, color, material, and labels. The lighting should assist this type of surface evaluation. After selecting an item, the customer will then usually wish to try it on or hold it against his body to see the fit. This viewing for fit is an outline evaluation, in which the customer is concerned with shape, bulges, alignment, and so on (fig. 6-3).

The designer must determine how the customer will need to evaluate a product and where this evaluation will take place. The lighting for each task

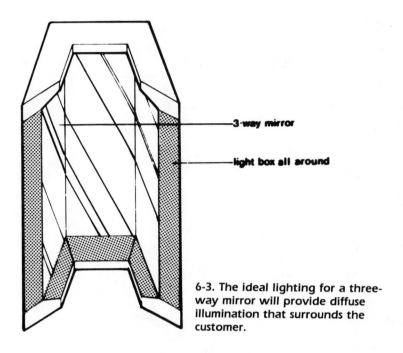

3-way mirror

light box all around

6-3. The ideal lighting for a three-way mirror will provide diffuse illumination that surrounds the customer.

category of product evaluation, surface or outline, requires different lighting solutions. However, some products are not evaluated visually. Perfume, for example, may be attractively displayed and this display may succeed in capturing the customer's interest, yet the purchase will not be completed until the customer tests the scent. Sight plays a small part in this customer evaluation. Similarly, the product evaluation of a pillow or mattress depends on the sense of touch, and a gourmet food store will close sales of its products with taste testing. Different aspects of the store design may play a stronger role than lighting in the evaluation of products by senses other than sight. However, lighting can still help to promote sales. If mattresses are being sold, the look of the product may not be as important as its touch, but the lighting can help sell the product by providing a quiet, restful environment.

Service Areas
Work areas and storage areas are the store's remaining lighting task areas. Back-room work areas may consist of alteration or tailoring spaces and wrapping, receiving, shipping, or business offices. Sales work areas include wrapping and cash counters and customer service areas. Stock and supplies may be stored within the sales area or in back rooms. These areas should be evaluated to determine lighting requirements. Offices and alteration or tailoring areas need high levels of shadow-free illumination, whereas storage and receiving areas need only moderate, uniform light.

LIGHTING CRITERIA

When a given area has been reviewed and designated as a specific lighting task area, the next step is to determine the appropriate lighting criteria for that area. Although there are a multitude of factors that may be considered as criteria, only those factors that relate to lighting sources will be discussed in this chapter. The three criteria for selecting lighting sources include: the color of the light source; the modeling effect; and the brightness of the light source.

Color

Light sources have a direct effect on the apparent color of merchandise displayed. This effect—the way that colors are perceived differently under different types of lighting—is called color rendering or metamerism. It is the designer's role to determine the optimum light source needed to achieve the appropriate color rendering of the product displayed or activity to be illuminated.

There is no "natural" or original color for a given product since its color will appear different under natural sunlight depending on the season, time of day, geographic location, the surrounding environment, and whether the sunlight is direct or indirect. Color also changes under artificial light, depending on whether the light source is incandescent, fluorescent, or high-intensity discharge. Each lighting task area must be evaluated to determine whether color rendering is important. Some of the situations that require accurate color rendering occur when there is a need to make color comparisons; there is a need to enhance or gray the color of the product; there is a need to simulate the color of an environment elsewhere; or there is a need to create a cool or warm store image.

The ability of a customer to make color comparisons may be a requirement in product-display areas, but may not be an issue in service areas if workers can distinguish different colored products by other means such as product number. However, in some service areas correct lighting may be critical. For example, a tailor must be able to match thread color correctly with material color in a suit of clothes. The human eye adapts to the color of a space and the light therein, whether warm or cold, will appear "white" in a short period of time. However, abrupt color changes between spaces in a store should be avoided since the eye adapts to the lighting of the first area and retains that state for a period of time in a new area. This could cause a salesperson coming from the back room with a different color lighting and a customer viewing a display to see two different colors for the same displayed product. Certain products, such as men's business clothing, typically colored in subdued, muted blues or grays, require a good color-discriminating environment. Other products, such as women's casual clothing, may be brightly colored and easy to distinguish under any lighting.

The colors of certain products may be enhanced (intensified) or grayed (made duller-looking) by using the proper light source. The spectral distribution of each light source is different, and the knowledge of how a given source distorts the color of a product permits the designer to change its color appearance. For example, such unwrapped food items as meat, coffee beans, and bread can be color enhanced under incandescent lighting, which accentuates the reds, browns, and yellows in the product color. Sometimes it is desirable to gray a product color, as for diamonds. Diamonds must appear clear white to be most marketable, but many diamonds have a yellow cast under warm light. Therefore, diamonds should be displayed under a cool light source that has a uniform spectral distribution, including the blue bands. This will tend to gray any yellow in the diamond. This practice is not deceptive if the product is presented in an artificial "white" light simulating natural lighting conditions; that is, north light, which is the jeweler's benchmark for color rendering. For feature display lighting, where dramatic effects are desired, colored lenses can be placed over light sources to enhance a product color to an unnatural extreme. This type of lighting is like theatrical lighting and will be required by a qualified show-window designer.

At times, it is important to display a product under a light source that accurately reflects the lighting conditions of the environment in which the product will later be used by the customer. This is the case with products like facial cosmetics. Make-up mirrors should permit the customer to adjust the lighting to reflect the various lighting conditions in which she may wear the cosmetics, such as daylight and office light. The lighting should offer a range of cool and warm lighting for product evaluation. In addition, products for use only in the home under natural or incandescent conditions—for example, furniture and furnishings—should be presented under neutral to warm lighting. This will reduce the possibility of customers returning products because they selected the wrong color.

Last, the color of the light source must be considered in terms of how it will affect the overall mood and image of a store. Warm lighting throughout the store in random light patterns will create an atmosphere of gaiety and intimacy while general cool lighting in a higher intensity will create a feeling of somberness and detachment (Nuckolls 1983, 354). The former may be appropriate in a toy store, and may be the most significant color-rending issue for that store, while the latter may be a major color-rendering factor in a financial institution or a store selling religious artifacts. Warm light also makes a store seem smaller and more intimate, while cool lighting enlarges the apparent size of a store.

Modeling

Modeling is lighting to create a three-dimensional effect in a product display. A completely diffuse light source eliminates all modeling effect, or shadow, whereas entirely direct light creates a severe modeling effect on a product (harsh shadow). Diffuse lighting is analogous to the flat, shadowless effect of daytime lighting in a fog; direct lighting produces the strong, delineated shadows of a single candle in a dark room.

Some retail lighting tasks require a great degree of modeling effect; others, none; and for some a combination of diffuse and direct lighting sources is the best solution. The designer must make this determination for each lighting task area. Display lighting, for example, often requires dramatic lighting, which can be created through modeling effect. Feature displays, too, are often very dramatically illuminated to accentuate the visual features of products beyond the normal lighting range (fig. 6-4). This is the nature of drama in display: colors are more colorful, textures richer, details sharper, and features sometimes revealed to the point of visual distortion. The intent of this dramatic lighting effect is to capture the customer's attention. Even products that are not modeled in product-evaluation areas may be modeled when in a feature display. A yellow cotton towel will appear significantly more interesting under a bright, direct, warm light source than under a bright, diffused, cool source. Within a properly designed display, it can become more than just a towel; it can become a work of art. Direct lighting is, therefore, useful for creating interesting, dramatic feature displays. It may also be used for merchandising displays (displays in which customers may handle the product). However, the designer must con-

6-4. High-intensity direct lighting of show-window feature displays provides visual drama.

sider the changes in lighting that will occur when the product is removed from the display for evaluation, which may remove the magic of controlled modeling. Often, the display lights must be used in the product-evaluation area as well, to prevent a great change in the appearance of the product when it is removed from the shelf. If this is not desirable, a contiguous feature display can be maintained as a visual reference point.

Even if dramatic effect is not desired, displays may be modeled simply to reveal the three-dimensional nature of a product or its interesting surface. In this case, a true representation of the product is desired. To achieve this effect, the designer will use a combination of direct and diffuse lighting to create the best normal (undramatic) lighting conditions (figs. 6-5, 6-6, and 6-7). This is the criterion for most store displays. The designer should strive to achieve natural but enhanced color, modeling, and brightness effects to present the product in its best light.

In product-evaluation areas, oblique shadows may be required to help the customer examine the texture or detail of a product, such as the fabric of a chair, the engraving on silverware, or the etching of clear glass. In other products, a three-dimensional effect will be needed for the customer to evaluate the outline of a sculpture, a flower, or a hat. Some products require little modeling effect for evaluation where other factors, such as color or intensity of light, are more significant. Linens, towels, carpeting, and other flat products usually fall into this category. For most work and storage areas, diffuse lighting is preferable, for the tasks to be illuminated, such as writing or using office machines, would not be aided by the introduction of shadows. Where demanding tasks are performed on machines, such as a tailor working on a sewing machine, shadowless diffuse light is essential.

Brightness

Lighting brightness can be viewed directly or indirectly. Direct or primary brightness is perceived when the viewer looks directly into the light source. Indirect or secondary brightness is the viewing of light reflected from a surface. Because secondary brightness is the most common brightness developed by the retail-store designer, it will be called simply "brightness" hereafter.

Brightness is a relative factor that depends on the following elements: the reflectivity of the object illuminated; the background contrast of the object; and the intensity of the light source. Brightness can range from dim to bright as perceived by the viewer and subject to the three elements of lighting listed above. The designer must determine the brightness level needed for each lighting task, within the range of dim to bright. Which areas of a retail store should appear bright to the shopper as he views the store? In most cases, of the three lighting task areas—display, product evaluation, and service—display areas should appear brighter than all other task areas, since the first objective of display is to focus the customer's attention on the merchandise. This approach of creating pools of brightness on displays is appropriate when merchandise attraction is the primary goal of lighting and the unique nature of the merchandise is the primary image of the store. However, if the store is selling price before uniqueness, the objective of lighting may be to provide a more uniform

6-5. *Above left:* Diffuse fluorescent soffit lighting alone provides no modeling effect.

6-6. *Above right:* Direct incandescent lighting provides good modeling but introduces objectionable shadows.

6-7. *Left:* The combination of diffuse and direct lighting provides a balanced product display with reduced shadowing.

level of brightness, emphasizing the merchandise, product evaluation, and service equally.

Each product to be illuminated has a certain reflectance, which depends on the product's color. White products reflect over 80 percent of the light illuminating them, whereas green or brown objects may reflect only 20 percent of the light. Photometric brightness—the degree of light intensity—can be measured with a photometer; the reflectance of the product will affect the level of brightness measured. Brightness measured from a reflecting surface is expressed in footlamberts, which may be estimated by multiplying the object's reflectance factor (the factor can be obtained from the photometric reading) by the number of footcandles produced by the light source.

The *quantity* of light emitted from a light source is measured in lumens. For example, a typical cool white, 40-watt fluorescent lamp has a normal output of 3,250 lumens. The *density* of light in a given area is measured in footcandles. Footcandles are determined by averaging the total lumens emitted over the area illuminated.

In other words, the brightness of a display is a factor of how much light is delivered to the display (footcandles) and how much is reflected back to the customer (footlamberts). Because light-colored objects have a greater reflectance factor, they will always appear brighter than dark-colored objects under the same light source with the same background. The designer should review the general color reflectance of merchandise to be displayed and these percentages of reflectivity should be noted on the design plan. If the designer does not have a photometer, he can use known reflective samples to estimate the reflectance factor of an item. Similarly, instead of trying to determine footcandles, the designer can consult a lighting manufacturer. Many lighting manufacturers provide charts (in their catalogs) from which the delivered footcandles of a light source can be estimated.

Products may also have a specular or mirrorlike quality. Light reflectance caused by a product's specular quality may either enhance or detract from the product. Enhancing reflections give a product sparkle and glitter and occur in glass, silver, jewelry, and similar products. Detracting reflections, known as veiling reflections, are caused by reflections in packaging materials and glass surfaces in front of products such as countertops and show windows. These reflections obscure product detail (figs. 6-8, 6-9). To eliminate undesirable reflections, the designer must position the light source so that it will not be reflected in the product displayed. Usually, this means locating the light source above or behind the customer. To increase reflections, where desirable, the opposite approach should be followed.

The second factor of brightness is background contrast. Background contrast (brightness ratio) is a strong factor in establishing the proper conditions for product evaluation. As noted, there are two categories of product evaluation: review of product surface, and review of product outline. If product surface must be examined, the contrast between the product and background should be minimized and the ratio of the reflectance of the product to the background should be less than 1:3. If the ratio is higher, the eye will adjust to the brighter background, which will obscure the detail of the product.

If the product outline is more important than the product's surface detail, the ratio of brightness can be increased, thereby revealing less detail but emphasizing the shape or form of the product. In this case, a light-colored product would be displayed against a dark background and vice versa. It should be noted that selecting the wrong background material can result in reflected

6-8. *Above:* Veiling reflections caused by light sources focused on a glass showcase distort the view into the product.

6-9. *Below:* Disturbing reflections have been eliminated by locating the light source inside and at the top of the showcase.

glare, which is the reflection of light sources by a background. Background materials, therefore, should have a matte finish no matter what its reflectance may be. Reflected glare will impair the customer's ability to see surface details or product outline.

The final factor of brightness is the light source, which affects brightness by its lumen output and concentration. Some light sources, such as incandescent reflector bulbs, are designed to concentrate light, while others, such as fluorescent tubes, do not. Light sources vary in their lumen output. The designer must determine the number of footcandles required for a given task area, considering many factors, such as the reflectance of the product; the background

SUGGESTED ILLUMINATION LEVELS (FOOTCANDLES)

Display Areas		Feature	200 - 500
		Merchandising	70 - 100
Product Evaluation		Surface	*50 - 100
		Outline	
Service-Work Area		Sales	50 - 75
		Office	75
		Alterations-Repair	125
		Stock	30
		Corridors-Aisles	30

*Higher levels may be required if product is removed from a highly illuminated area.

6-10. Recommended illumination levels for retail-store task areas.

surrounding a product; and the brightness of all other areas within or outside the store in relation to the task area.

Suggested illumination levels, as shown in figure 6-10, may assist the designer in determining the footcandle level to be maintained in the various areas of the store. However, these illumination levels should be used only as a relative guide, since each store will have its own requirements. The designer should also bear in mind the following general guidelines for brightness:

1. Feature displays should have a brightness 5 to 10 times that of nearby surfaces.
2. If a noticeable transition from one area to another is desirable, one space should be 10 times brighter than another. If only a break in lighting continuity from space to space is required, the ratio should be at least 3:1.
3. If lighting continuity is required, a ratio less than 3:1 should be maintained.
4. Color discrimination will be lost at levels below 10 footlamberts (Illuminating Engineering Society of North America 1976).

LIGHTING SOURCES

The discussion that follows will be restricted to artificial, nondecorative light sources. Retail stores are similar to legitimate theaters in their lighting needs: both require precise lighting control to dramatize the environment. This control is most easily attained by excluding natural light, rather than by attempting to modulate it. While there may be times in which natural light is necessary, for reasons such as cost-efficiency or psychology, the techniques of controlling sunlight to achieve the best possible lighting of each task area during the day and evening are beyond the scope of this book.

Once the designer has identified the lighting task areas within the store and determined the lighting criteria for each area, the lighting source for each area must be selected based on these criteria. Each lighting source has three basic components: the lamp, the fixture, and the location of the source in relation to the task. Each component has an effect on the color rendering, modeling, and brightness of the area to be illuminated.

For example, if the task area is a men's suit display, the designer may have determined lighting criteria calling for accurate, blue-spectrum color rendering; diffuse lighting of the suit surface; and moderate brightness without glare. The lighting source selected might then be a cool white deluxe fluorescent lamp with a single lamp and a metal tube fixture, to be located in front of the suits. By knowing the various properties of each lighting source, correct selections can be made.

Filament Lamps

The incandescent lamp consists of a wire filament sealed in glass containing an inert gas or enclosing a vacuum. When electrical current is passed through the wire, it heats to the point of incandescence and emits light. The lamp (or bulb) should not be confused with the fixture that houses it.

Incandescent lamps all have similar color-rendering properties. They emit a warm, yellow-white light that is very flattering to human skin color, that is bright and cheerful, and that enhances the red/yellow range of colors. It is, however, a very poor light in which to discriminate blues, blacks, and greens—colors tend to gray. Tungsten, halogen gas incandescent lamps provide a more balanced color rendering than typical argon and nitrogen gas incandescent sources.

Incandescent lamps used in retail stores to illuminate a task (as opposed to

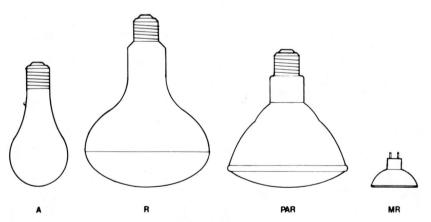

A   R   PAR   MR

6-11. The shapes and names of bulbs commonly used in retail stores.

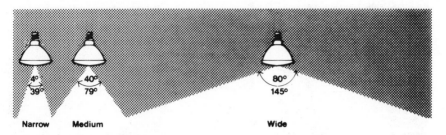

Narrow Medium Wide

6-12. Directional bulbs are available in various beam spreads.

decoration) fall into two basic modeling categories: diffuse or directional (fig. 6-11). Diffuse incandescent lamps are either A-bulbs (arbitrary shape) or P-bulbs (pear shape). These bulbs are housed in fixtures that may reflect their light directionally or diffusely. A- and P-bulbs are inexpensive to replace, have a rated life of about 1,000 hours, and are filled with argon and nitrogen. In addition to A- and P-bulbs, directional incandescent lamps include R-bulbs (reflector); PAR-bulbs (parabolic aluminized reflector); and MR-bulbs (multi-faceted open reflector). R- and PAR-bulbs are filled with argon and nitrogen; PAR-bulbs may also contain tungsten filaments and halogen-gas lamps. MR-bulbs are exclusively tungsten filament halogen-gas lamps. These three bulb types (MR, R, and PAR) have built-in reflectors that direct light and do not require reflectors in the fixture housing. The interiors of R-and PAR-bulbs are silvered to create this reflector, while the MR-bulb consists of a tungsten filament, halogen-gas lamp that operates at low voltage and is attached to a small mirrored reflector. MR-bulbs require a transformer to reduce voltage for their operation. R-, PAR-, and MR-bulbs are more expensive to replace than A- or P-bulbs, but R- and PAR-bulbs have a rated life of about 2,000 hours; MR-bulbs have a rated life of 2,500 to 3,500 hours, depending on wattage.

Beam spread is the shape and size of the light emitted by a lamp. Directional bulbs are available in various beam spreads, including WFL (wide flood), FL (flood), MFL (medium flood), SP (spot), NSP (narrow spot), and VNSP (very narrow spot) (fig. 6-12). These spreads may range from 4 to 145 degrees, depending on the type of bulb, and they may take a circular or oval configuration (fig. 6-13).

Incandescent lamps produce 17 to 22 lumens per watt, whereas fluorescent lamps produce 67 to 83 lumens per watt. While incandescent lamps are less efficient than fluorescent and other discharge-type lamps are (the more lumens per watt, the greater the efficiency), directional incandescent lamps are capable of lighting display areas effectively and precisely, in a manner unmatched by discharge lamps. In addition, incandescent lamps are available in a wide range of brightnesses, and can be dimmed (with dimmer controls) at a reasonable expense. Therefore, if the lighting criteria for a task area call for warm color rendering and/or precise directional modeling effect, incandescent lamps should be used.

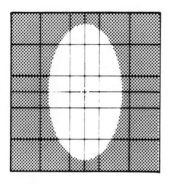

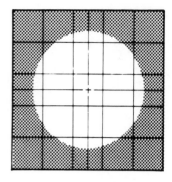

Oval Pattern   **Circular Pattern**

6-13. Directional bulbs have two common lighting patterns. The oval pattern may be useful for lighting a rectangular surface.

Discharge Lamps

There are two types of discharge lamps, fluorescent and high-intensity discharge (HID).

Fluorescent lamps are glass tubes coated on the inside with phosphor and filled with a low-pressure, inert gas and a small amount of mercury vapor. Inside each end of the tube are electrodes that act as terminals for an electric arc, which excites the atoms of the mercury vapor to release ultraviolet radiation, which, in turn, activates the phosphor and emits visible light. These lamps are relatively inexpensive to replace and are rated for a life of approximately 9,000 to 20,000 hours. Fluorescent lamps require an electrical ballast to control the electrical currrent to the lamp; each fixture comes equipped with the necessary ballast.

The color rendering of fluorescent lamps depends on the type of phosphorous fluorescent material applied to the inside surface of the tube (fig. 6-14). If excellent color rendering is required and lamp efficiency (lumens per watt) is not an issue, the designer should select either warm white deluxe, cool white deluxe, Chroma 50 or Chroma 75 (C50 or C75). While these lamps all give excellent color rendering, they vary in their "warmness," with deluxe warm white on the warm end of the scale and C75 at the cool end. Although all are appropriate for retail store use, the choice depends on the merchandise for sale. Colorful women's wear will look better under warm white deluxe, men's suits under cool white deluxe, flowers under cool white deluxe or C50, and crystal and glassware under C75. If lamp and cost-efficiency are factors, warm light deluxe, white deluxe, or light white deluxe should be used.

Fluorescent lamps are nondirectional, diffuse lighting sources and will provide little modeling effect. With regard to brightness, fluorescent lamps are very efficient light sources, using up to 80 percent less energy than incandescent

COLOR RENDITION OF FLUORESCENT LAMPS

Lamp	Colors Enhanced	Colors Grayed	Appearance	Color Rendition
cool white deluxe CWX	all	none	white(pinkish)	excellent-simulates cloudy day
warm white deluxe WWX	red, orange, yellow, green	blue	yellowish	simulates incandescent
cool white CX	blue, green, orange	yellow, red	white (bluish)	fair
warm white WW	yellow, red	blue	yellow-white	fair
warm light deluxe WLX	red, orange	deep red, blue	yellowish	good
white deluxe WX	red, orange, green	deep red	yellowish	good
light white deluxe LWX	red, orange, green, blue	deep red	pale greenish	good
C50	all	none	white (bluish)	simulates partly cloudy day
C75	all	none	bluish white	simulates north sky light

6-14. Color rendition of fluorescent lamps.

sources. They should be used in conjunction with incandescent lights to achieve a balance of diffuse and directional light. One advantage to using fluorescent lamps is that they increase lighting levels (67 to 83 lumens per watt) without creating the problem of heat gain associated with incandescent lighting. They illuminate large areas efficiently and have very long rated lives compared to incandescent lamps. Fluorescent lamps are dimmable, but the dimmer systems required are expensive.

High-intensity discharge (HID) lamps are similar to fluorescent lamps in operation and efficiency, and to incandescent lamps in shape and size. The gas vapor is either mercury, metal halide with mercury, or high-pressure sodium. These lamps have a rated life of about 20,000 hours and, like fluorescent lamps, they also require a ballast to control the electrical current to the lamp. Color-corrected metal halide lamps, such as the General Electric Multi Vapor II, do not have the smooth spectral distribution of an incandescent or deluxe fluorescent lamp and, therefore, are less able to provide accurate color rendering. However, they might be suitable for hardware stores or other retail stores where color rendering is less important. Uncorrected metal halide lamps tend to gray reds and enhance blues, greens, and yellows.

HID lamps can be used to provide general diffuse illumination. In open-reflector-type fixtures, these lamps can give some of the appearance and modeling effect of incandescent lighting. In terms of brightness, metal halide lamps are even more efficient (85 to 115 lumens per watt) than fluorescent lamps. They may be used if the cost of lighting is a strong factor, but should be avoided if color rendering is essential. They are dimmable, but, as for fluorescent lamps, the dimmers are more expensive than dimmers for incandescent systems. In addition, HID fixtures require a warm-up period of several minutes before they reach full lighting intensity.

FIXTURES

There are two basic types of light fixtures used in retail stores: direct and indirect. Direct lighting fixtures aim light directly on the task, whereas indirect lighting fixtures direct light toward the ceiling or soffit above, either of which then reflects this light down to the task below. Direct lighting can be either diffuse or directional; indirect lighting is invariably diffuse.

Direct Lighting Fixtures

The following direct lighting fixtures are categorized by fixtures that permit the installation of more than one type of lamp: recessed, open reflector, nonreflector, and adjustable downlights; wall washers; track lighting; troffers; and pendant and surface-mounted fixtures.

Recessed downlights, the first type of fixture, are installed above the ceiling with only a small trim ring left exposed below the ceiling (fig. 6-15). They are manufactured for general-service (A- and P-bulbs) and reflector incandescent lamps and for HID lamps. The light output from these fixtures is directed almost totally downward.

Open-reflector downlights are the least complicated of the downlights. They consist of a simple metal fixture with a socket that houses a general-service lamp or HID lamp (for HID fixtures, a ballast is also provided), and a dome-shaped reflector to redirect the light from the lamp. A common reflector for this type is a specular Alzak, a highly polished, dome-shaped reflector that is available in a clear or gold finish (fig. 6-16). Open reflectors provide excellent general lighting with some modeling effect. They offer easy lamp maintenance

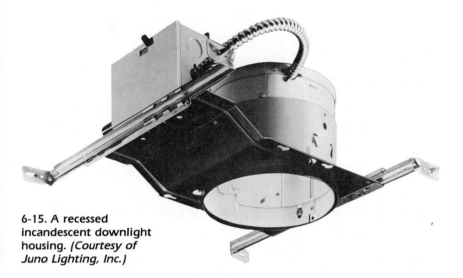

**6-15. A recessed
incandescent downlight
housing. *(Courtesy of
Juno Lighting, Inc.)***

(no parts need be removed to get to the lamp, and the reflector can be removed with an extension pole), full dimming capability, and reasonable direct glare control. For further glare control, open-reflector downlights are available with different low-brightness trim rings that extend up into the fixture. These trim rings may be grooved or have a nonreflective finish. In either case, the direct glare is eliminated for normal viewing angles.

Nonreflector downlights consists of a fully recessed metal housing with a socket to receive a lamp. A transformer is also provided if the downlight uses low-voltage MR-bulbs (fig. 6-17). The lamp must have its own reflector system since none is provided in the fixture itself. Therefore, nonreflector downlights

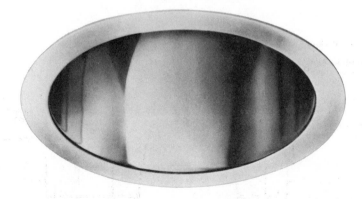

6-16. A specular Alzak reflector. *(Courtesy of Juno Lighting, Inc.)*

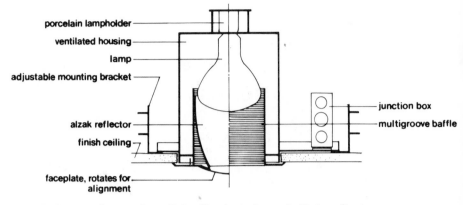

porcelain lampholder
ventilated housing
lamp
adjustable mounting bracket
alzak reflector
finish ceiling
faceplate, rotates for alignment
junction box
multigroove baffle

6-17. A nonreflector downlight. The lamp has a built-in reflector.

are designed to house R-, PAR-, or MR-bulbs, all of which have built-in reflector systems. These fixtures may also use low-brightness grooved or nonreflective baffles mounted between the lamp and the bottom of the fixture. Nonreflector downlight fixtures offer low initial cost and can provide directional light as well as a great degree of modeling effect, depending on the lamp used. Lamp replacement is expensive and difficult (the lamps cannot be removed with poles), but there is the advantage of having a new optical system installed with each replacement.

Adjustable downlights consist of a metal housing that is either fully recessed into the ceiling (open adjustable type) or semirecessed (the "eyeball" type) (fig. 6-18). Each type has an adjustable socket and uses lamps with internal reflector systems: R-, PAR-, or MR-bulbs. These light sources provide unobtrusive, glare-free, directional light and can be adjusted to illuminate objects that are not located directly below the fixture—the lamp can be rotated almost 360

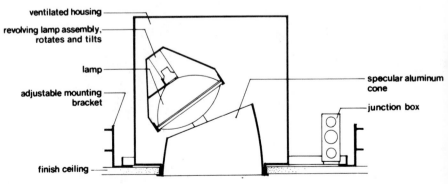

ventilated housing
revolving lamp assembly, rotates and tilts
lamp
adjustable mounting bracket
specular aluminum cone
junction box
finish ceiling

6-18. A recessed, adjustable downlight.

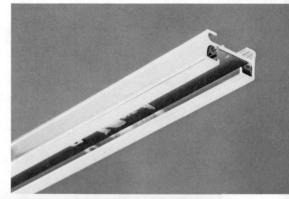

6-19. Cross section of a light track.
(Courtesy of Juno Lighting, Inc.)

6-20. A wide variety of track lighting fixtures are available.
(Courtesy of Juno Lighting, Inc.)

degrees and can tilt up to 35 degrees. These fixtures have the same maintenance qualities as nonreflector downlights—that is, the lamps are expensive and difficult to replace.

Wall washers consist of a fully recessed metal housing that has a fixed socket with or without a built-in reflector. Therefore, they can house both reflector and nonreflector lamps. They are designed to be located in a series along, and about three feet away from, the wall and one another. When properly installed, they cast even, diffuse illumination on the wall; they do not direct light onto horizontal surfaces below except by reflectance.

Track lighting is derived from theater lighting, and is a system of direct lighting fixtures that are fully exposed, fully adjustable, and may be relocated anywhere along the track—a continuous linear electrical power source and hanging system (fig. 6-19). Track lighting fixtures use reflector lamps, R-, PAR-, or MR-bulbs, and MR track lights also have integral solid-state transformers. A wide variety of fixture housings are available to the designer (fig. 6-20). Most vary simply in style, color, and material.

Track lighting offers a great degree of flexibility to the designer, since not only the direction of the light can be changed, but also its location. This feature

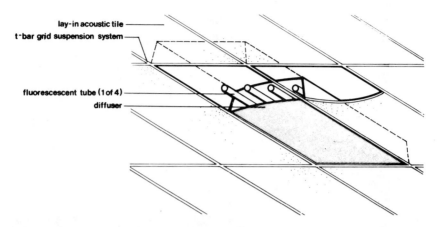

lay-in acoustic tile
t-bar grid suspension system

fluorescescent tube (1 of 4)
diffuser

6-21. Cut-away view of a fluorescent troffer.

makes track lighting an ideal auxiliary or primary lighting source for a retail store. Track lights are also available with colored filters that attach directly to the fixture. The biggest drawback to track lights is the potential direct-glare problem. Since the lights can be positioned in any direction, it is likely the light source will be visible and produce glare. Some baffles are available to control glare. These cause the lamp to be recessed deep into the fixture. Even though this effectively cuts off light, store personnel must be instructed to be aware of the problem of direct glare and the fixtures must always be positioned to control this problem.

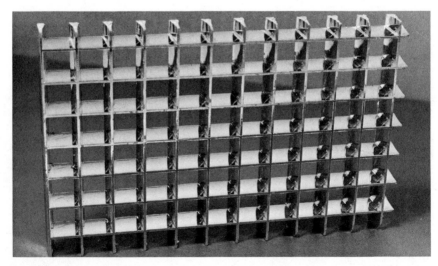

6-22. Parabolic section louvers can be used to control the glare of fluorescent lighting.

6-23. Fluorescent soffit light with parabolic section louver. *(Photography: Karant & Associates, Inc.)*

6-24. Vertical section of a fluorescent soffit light.

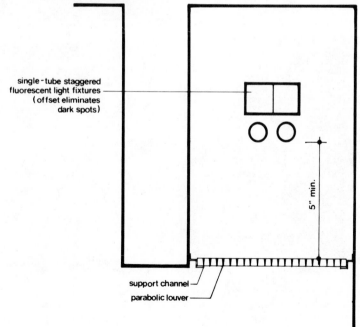

single-tube staggered fluorescent light fixtures (offset eliminates dark spots)

5" min.

support channel

parabolic louver

Troffers are metal boxes that can be fully recessed into the ceiling. They are square or rectangular, house and connect ballasts and one to four fluorescent tubes, and have a lens through which light passes (fig. 6-21). Troffers are an economical means of providing general diffuse illumination. However, the biggest problem associated with them is glare. Although the lamps are concealed, the lens at the ceiling plane becomes a source of glare and tends to draw the customer's eyes up, away from the merchandise. Special lenses, like parabolic section louvers, are available to control this surface brightness (fig. 6-22). These louvers are of the egg-carton type, with cells approximately ½ inch square and deep that have special optical properties to reduce wasted light and direct it downward. This results in a fixture that appears dark when the lamps are lit. These lens are more expensive than other typical acrylic, prismatic lenses, but offer the complete elimination of the direct glare problem (figs. 6-23, 6-24).

Pendant and surface-mounted fixtures have fully exposed and finished housings. Pendants are suspended from the ceiling on rods and are used where ceilings are high, requiring fixtures to be lower, or where ceilings are unfinished. Surface-mounted fixtures are attached directly to a ceiling or soffit and are exposed to view. These fixtures may be used on unfinished ceilings or as an architectural feature. Pendant and surface-mounted fixtures have design and

6-25. Indirect lighting provides glare-free, general diffuse illumination.
(Design: Sumner Schein Architects and Engineers; electrical engineering, Edwin P. Mahard, Inc.; photography: Schlowsky Studios)

optical qualities similar to the direct lighting, recessed, and track light fixtures discussed earlier.

Indirect Light Fixtures

Indirect lighting is used to achieve general diffuse illumination (fig. 6-25). Light is directed toward the ceiling and reflected onto the task area below: the lighting effect is uniform and diffuse. Indirect lighting is often used in conjunction with directional lighting sources because it is totally diffuse and provides no modeling effect. The color rendering of the fixture depends on both the lamp used and the color of the ceiling surface that reflects the light. Care must be taken not to attempt intense lighting levels or extreme ceiling brightness will result, detracting from the merchandise.

Indirect pendant fixtures are fully exposed and finished fixtures suspended 18 to 36 inches below and directed up toward a ceiling. These may use incandescent, fluorescent, or HID lamps (fig. 6-26).

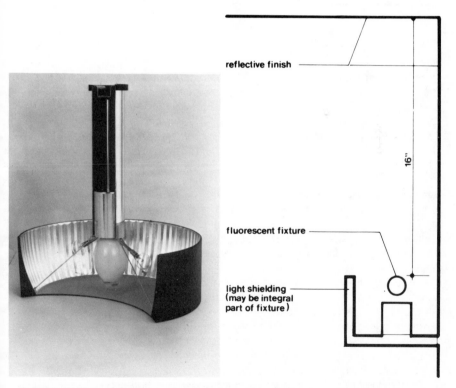

6-26. *Left:* **Cut-away view of a high-intensity-discharge pendant lamp fixture.**

6-27. *Right:* **Vertical section of a typical cove fixture for an indirect fluorescent lamp.**

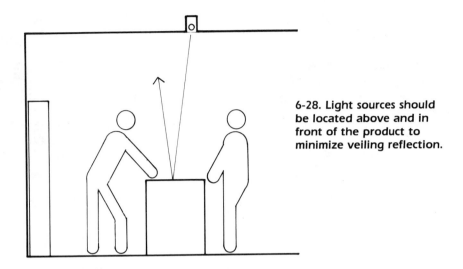

6-28. Light sources should be located above and in front of the product to minimize veiling reflection.

Cove and bracket fixtures and sconces are wall mounted 18 to 36 inches below a ceiling. These may use fluorescent or incandescent lamps (fig. 6-27). Cove fixtures provide indirect light and are suitable for general illumination. They are composed of fixtures hidden behind a cove molding or a decorative linear box. Brackets and sconces are individual fixtures mounted onto walls. They can provide either directed or indirect light, and are usually used for decorative purposes. Floor- or store-fixture-mounted light fixtures may use fluorescent, incandescent, or HID lamps. These are typically used with low ceilings, which do not permit the use of pendant fixtures.

Locating Light Sources
In most cases, lighting sources for product displays should be located in front of and above the product to be illuminated. There are two reasons for this positioning: it creates a natural lighting effect similar to natural lighting; and it minimizes direct glare from the fixture, since it is aimed away from the viewer. Because the light reflected from a horizontal case bounces up and away from the viewer, veiling reflections are also reduced (fig. 6-28). If light is reflected from a vertical case, it will bounce toward the viewer's feet. For similar reasons, this position is also frequently used for product-evaluation and service areas. However, there are times when it may be desirable to illuminate from below or even behind a displayed product. A product may appear more interesting or sculptured when illuminated from below; clear vases and glass art, for example, transmit light from below and seem luminous. Light from below can also make products appear more dramatic or unusual simply because they are rarely displayed in that manner. Light can be used to wash the surface behind a product, thereby silhouetting the product's outline. This type of lighting placement can be used in conjunction with a directional light source in front of and above the product, to show surface detail as well as outline. If product

outline is the key to its sale and surface is less important, back lighting can be used alone.

Other factors of source location include the relationship of one source to another for the creation of uniform lighting distribution, and the number of sources required to achieve a certain lighting brightness. It is beyond the scope of this discussion to detail the characteristics of each manufacturer's lighting fixtures, or the method of spacing fixtures for uniform illumination or to create a desired lighting brightness level. The designer should secure such information from the lighting manufacturer or consult a lighting engineer.

SEVEN

SYSTEMS

PLUMBING

Plumbing may or may not be required in a retail store, depending on the store's operational needs. The most common plumbing installation in a retail store is employee washrooms. This may entail installing one or two water closets, depending on the number of employees; some jurisdictions may require these to be handicap-accessible. The requirement for employee lavatories is sometimes waived if the landlord provides adequate public washrooms for both shoppers and employees. However, it is generally better business practice to install at least one washroom in the store, to avoid the need of closing the store during the day if it is operated by one person.

Other plumbing requirements of a retail store may include a sink for hand washing, an employee kitchen sink, or a utility sink for cleaning tools or watering plants. A floor or wall drain and waste line will have to be provided to accommodate HVAC condensate or sprinkler-system drain water.

Service and Equipment

In most shopping centers, the tenant's space will be provided with plumbing stub-ins or connections. Water meters may be located within a tenant space or in a separate meter room. Remote meter-reading devices in the service corridor or on an exterior wall may be required if the meter is located within the store. Cold water and vent lines are generally extended to the rear of the store, along with waste lines located there below the floor. The tenant completes the installation within the store and connects to these stub-ins. Overhead waste and water pipes should be properly insulated to prevent damage from condensation. The landlord's intention in bringing these services to the store is to minimize disruption of other tenants' businesses while the plumbing is being installed in the new tenant's store. To minimize damage from overflow, the floor of a washroom or sink area should be waterproofed if the store is above another store. Usually, the landlord will not pour concrete for a lavatory floor at grade, but will leave this area open to facilitate the plumbing installation. If additional w.c. facilities are required that extend outside the open area provided, the concrete in these areas must be sawed and removed so that additional sanitary lines can be installed. This is often the case in restaurant installations. Other piping, such as water and vent, may be run overhead. If the tenant space is on an upper level of the shopping mall, the tenant may be forced to install plumbing on the premises of the tenant located below. If this is the case, this work should be carefully planned, scheduled, and executed with the lower store properly protected to prevent damage or disruption of its operations. Waste-line cleanouts should be located in the floor of the space served by the line, not in the ceiling of the space below. In this way, if the line must be cleaned out, no other tenants will be inconvenienced.

If a tenant needs hot water for a sink or lavatory, he may install a small (6- to 12-gallon) electric water heater either above the ceiling or in a vanity cabinet. The water heater will require an overflow drain, which may be a separate funnel drain or may be piped to overflow in a lavatory, depending on local codes.

The plumbing fixtures typically installed in retail stores consist of a stainless-steel bar sink for small counters used as kitchens, a garbage disposal and grease trap, if food will be present, and a wall-hung toilet, if special facilities are required for people with limited mobility. Using the wall-hung toilet fixture will permit the washroom to remain a minimum size, since, unlike a vanity lavatory, a wheelchair can roll under the wall-hung toilet. Urinals are not often installed in retail stores except in larger washrooms. A floor drain is desirable and should be installed even if not required by code. The advantage of such a drain in a plumbing emergency, such as a fire-protection sprinkler activation, is obvious. Water coolers or drinking fountains are usually not provided except in the largest stores.

FIRE PROTECTION

Sprinkler Systems

While in-line and freestanding stores may not require it, almost all shopping malls have a fire-protection sprinkler system. Tenants of shopping-mall stores will be required to connect to these systems, and install an internal layout of sprinklers that conforms to local building codes and satisfies the landlord's insurance underwriters. Some malls provide complete systems, including a grid of sprinkler heads. The tenant will then be required to modify the location of sprinkler heads in accordance with the requirements of the space.

A wet-pipe fire-protection system is a network of piping and sprinkler heads throughout the building. The system is filled with pressurized water; in a fire, the sprinkler heads will release a spray of water and extinguish the flames.

Except for those in very small buildings, the sprinkler system is usually isolated from other water systems in the building. Pressure in the system is maintained by pumps.

The design of sprinkler systems is generally governed by the standards of the National Fire Protection Association. Their pamphlet, NFPA 13, offers a full explanation of their requirements, which dictate the maximum area of sprinkler-head coverage (area requirements) and maximum and minimum spacing between heads and from heads to partitions. For the benefit of the tenant's designer, the landlord's lease usually spells out the area requirements for the building.

Building sprinkler systems will have some form of monitoring device to notify building personnel and fire fighters where an activated head is located. These monitoring devices are called flow alarms. The landlord may install flow alarms in a main riser or major supply line or the tenant may install one in or near his storefront. The signal from the alarm may go to a central monitoring location in the mall, may go straight to the fire department, or may activate a signal light at the storefront, or some combination of these. In any event, the building system's requirements will dictate whether a flow alarm should be installed by the tenant. Before a sprinkler system is accepted by the landlord's insurance underwriter, it must be tested for a period of time at excessive water pressures. Once the test is completed successfully, the new system will be activated as part of the building system. Sprinkler systems must be coordinated with ventilating and lighting systems to avoid conflicts.

The most significant design feature of a sprinkler system is the sprinkler head. These heads are generally all that is visible because the remainder of the system is concealed above the ceiling or in partitions. The sprinkler head is mounted in the wall or ceiling and connected to the sprinkler supply piping. If the room reaches a high temperature (usually 165°F), the sprinkler head will spray the nearby area with water and extinguish the fire. Many different types of heads are available, but from a design standpoint there are three to be considered for exposed locations in a retail store. The first and least expensive is the pendant type (fig. 7-1). The pendant head is the industry standard and is used widely, but presents a problem for design-sensitive projects (the pendant head is not as attractive as some of the others). The flush pendant type, as shown in figure 7-2, is slightly more expensive than the simple pendant type, but is recessed into the ceiling and so is less visible. In the concealed sprinkler head, as shown in figure 7-3, the only visible element is a plate flush with the ceiling. This plate can be painted at the factory to match any ceiling color, and offers a neutral design image.

Fire Extinguishers

Local codes or the community fire department will require the tenant to install fire extinguishers. The exact number and type required will vary, but at least one all-purpose extinguisher should be placed in the storeroom or other non-public area. Specific requirements are detailed by the National Fire Protection Association, pamphlet #10.

7-1. Pendant sprinkler head.
*(Courtesy of Star Sprinkler
Corporation)*

7-2. Flush pendant sprinkler head.
*(Courtesy of Star Sprinkler
Corporation)*

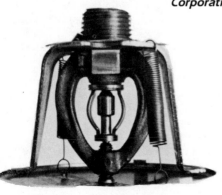

7-3. Concealed sprinkler head.
*(Courtesy of Star Sprinkler
Corporation)*

Smoke and Heat Detectors

Smoke and heat detectors are not typically required to be installed within a retail store. However, in some buildings having central HVAC systems, they may be required to be installed within a return duct. In the event of a fire, the HVAC system will operate at one-hundred-percent exhaust and thereby not recirculate smoke developed.

HEATING, VENTILATING, AND AIR CONDITIONING SYSTEMS

Heating, ventilating, and air conditioning (HVAC) systems for buildings that house retail stores are generally designed with flexibility in mind. The system must be able to accommodate a variety of lighting, equipment, and traffic loads within a space. In addition, the system must be able to adapt to the constant subdivision and expansion of individual retail spaces within a shopping center. System solutions to these problems have been the multizone central station system and the variable air volume system. Both of these systems are very flexible, and rely on the landlord's building system, which supplies either treated air or water to a local distribution point. In general, these systems are used only in larger shopping centers. Individual buildings, smaller shopping centers, and strip centers generally use rooftop HVAC units, which do not offer the flexibility of the more sophisticated systems, but are substantially less expensive.

Central Station Systems

In a central station system, hot or cold water is piped into the individual retail store from the shopping-center landlord's building system. This hot and cold water piping is often stubbed into the tenant's space and capped. In addition, the landlord typically supplies the tenant with a fresh-air duct or directs the tenant to a location or duct that connects to an outside air source. The tenant usually installs the central station air-handling unit and all distribution ductwork and controls. The central station air-handling unit is a packaged unit, a rectilinear metal box containing dampers to mix outside air with return air, and an electric supply fan and coils that disperse heat and cool air supplied by the landlord's building system (fig. 7-4). Commonly, one central station air-handling unit acts as a local heating/cooling unit for a single store. The unit permits total control of the store environment, modulated by a store thermostat.

The central station air handler operates as follows: outside and return (recirculated) air is drawn into the unit, mixed, and filtered; this blended air passes through the fan and is blown across the heating and cooling coils; and the treated air is discharged through a dampered discharge that controls the air volume and distributes it through the store (fig. 7-5).

Variable Air Volume Systems

In a variable air volume system, cool supply air is ducted into the tenant's retail store from the landlord's building system. The tenant connects the system to this duct and provides the variable air volume (VAV) terminal or box and all distribution ductwork and controls. The cool air may be a combination of out-

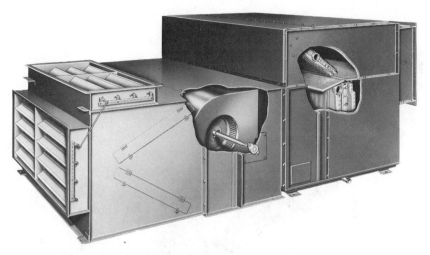

7-4. Cut-away view of a central station air-handling unit. *(Courtesy of the Trane Company)*

side and recirculated air, or may be only outside air. It may be filtered and tempered with heat, if necessary, or chilled to achieve an approximate temperature of 55°F.

The type of VAV terminal that is generally used is the induction terminal (fig. 7-6). This rectilinear metal box is mounted above the ceiling and draws warmed air from the ceiling return air plenum (the space above the ceiling) or from return ducts in the retail store into the box. The return air is then mixed with the conditioned primary supply air from the landlord's building system and controlled by motorized dampers within the induction terminal. These dampers, in turn, are regulated by store thermostats to maintain the desired

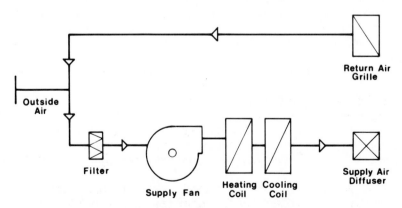

7-5. The components of a central station air-handling system.

7-6. A VAV terminal: induction box. *(Courtesy of the Barber-Colman Company)*

ambient temperature. If more cooling is called for by the thermostats, the primary air dampers will open wider and the induced air dampers will close down to a minimum. If less cooling is required, the primary air dampers will shut to a minimum and the induced air dampers will open wide (fig. 7-7).

Return air is warmed by the people, equipment, and lighting loads in the retail store. If a ceiling plenum return is used, the air in this plenum is also heated by heat from recessed ceiling-mounted light fixtures. If the combination of warmed return air and conditioned supply air will not be sufficient to warm the store, electric heaters are mounted at the induction box to provide supplementary heat when necessary. The use of the electric heaters is usually required only in the first hours of store operation, until all the stores are warmed. After that, the return air is sufficiently warm to maintain desired heating levels.

Rooftop Packaged Units
Rooftop HVAC units are typically used in one-story-high shopping centers, and are less expensive than a total building HVAC system. If the landlord supplies the unit, the tenant provides all distribution ductwork and controls. However, the tenant may be required to provide the entire system, including the rooftop unit.

The rooftop unit is an air-cooled, local, self-contained unit often set on a prefabricated roof curb (fig. 7-8). One or more rooftop units will furnish all the heating, ventilating, and cooling required by the retail store. The unit contains

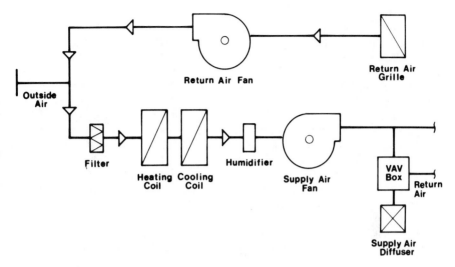

7-7. The components of VAV induction box system.

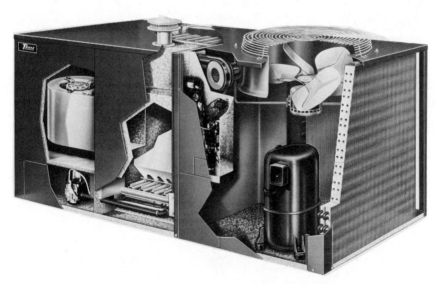

7-8. Cut-away view of a rooftop packaged HVAC unit. *(Courtesy of the Trane Company)*

all the components of the refrigeration cycle: compressor, condenser, and evaporator. In the refrigeration cycle, the compressor supplies heat to Freon in its liquid state, which converts the heat to a vapor. As this vapor enters the condenser, air is passed over the coils containing the gas, which removes heat from the gas and converts it to a cooled liquid. This cooled liquid then passes to the evaporator coils; primary supply air is passed over the coils and the heat in the air is absorbed into the liquid, converting it into a gas; and the cycle is repeated (fig. 7-9). Thus, the cooled supply air is ducted into the retail store, and return air is ducted back to the rooftop unit and mixed with the supply air. Thermostats located in the store regulate the operation of the unit.

Heating, when required, may be provided by gas-fired burners or electrical coils in the HVAC unit or the duct system. Or, a separate heat source or furnace, known as a split system, is used in some two-story malls (fig. 7-10). The furnace, fan, and evaporator are located in the tenant space while the cooling compressor, which pipes chilled refrigerant into the tenant space, is located on the roof. The adequacy of the building structure supporting a rooftop unit must be determined, and, if inadequate, the structure must be reinforced.

Water-Cooled Packaged Units

Water-cooled, self-contained packaged units are typically used in multistoried buildings. Usually, the landlord furnishes the tenant with a ducted outside air connection, a capped connection source, and the return of condenser water to the tenant's space. The tenant provides the packaged unit and all distribution ductwork and controls. The components and operation of the water-cooled packaged unit are similar to that of the rooftop packaged unit, except that water instead of air is used to condense the refrigerant. This water is supplied by the building system's remotely located cooling tower. If heating is required, electric duct or strip heaters must be supplied (usually by the tenant). Water-cooled packaged units are available in horizontal and vertical units. Horizontal units may be installed above ceilings, whereas vertical units are generally floor-mounted in back rooms.

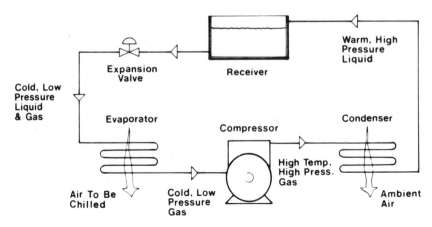

7-9. The refrigeration cycle.

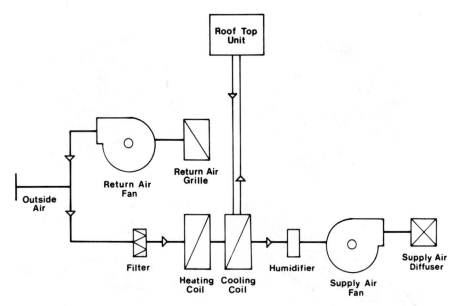

7-10. A split system separates the heating unit in the store from the cooling unit on the roof. *(Source: Robert Miskinis)*

Ducts

Retail-store ducts are commonly constructed of galvanized sheet metal and run above the ceiling. Supply- and return-air ducts connect the air-handling unit to the space, although return-air ducts may be eliminated if the ceiling plenum is used as a return-air chamber. Although ducts are usually made of galvanized sheet metal, ducts exposed to the weather may be aluminum, and ducts that are part of a kitchen exhaust system will be constructed of black iron. Flexible reinforced-plastic ducts may be used for the last few feet of supply ductwork or the first few feet of return ductwork, to permit ease of location for diffusers or registers.

Dampers

Dampers are installed in supply-air ducts to control the volume of air flow. These dampers are separate and independent from local registers set behind supply-air diffusers. In an inaccessible ceiling, such as one made of gypsum board, access panels must be provided so that workmen can reach the dampers without difficulty. The ceiling pads of an accessible ceiling, such as one made of acoustical tile, may be removed to provide access. Access panels are not necessary if Young regulators or similar remote-control devices are used. These consist of simple rods that extend from the ceiling surface to the damper, and may be operated by a tool inserted into the ceiling.

Supply Diffusers and Return Registers

Supply diffusers distribute supply air from the duct to the conditioned space, and contain local volume controls. Diffusers should be placed so that they do

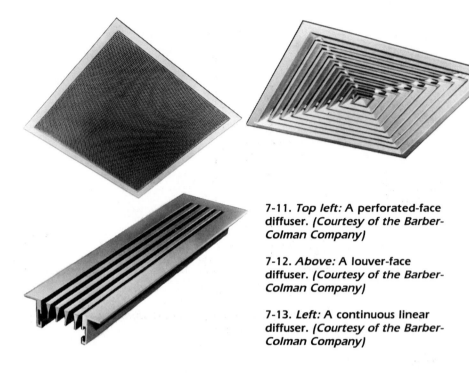

7-11. *Top left:* A perforated-face diffuser. *(Courtesy of the Barber-Colman Company)*

7-12. *Above:* A louver-face diffuser. *(Courtesy of the Barber-Colman Company)*

7-13. *Left:* A continuous linear diffuser. *(Courtesy of the Barber-Colman Company)*

not direct drafts on shoppers or employees. Three common types of supply diffusers include the perforated face, louver face, and the continuous linear type (figs. 7-11, 7-12, and 7-13). All are designed to be incorporated into a gypsum-board or plaster ceiling or a ceiling grid system. Linear types are more expensive to install than are perforated or louver-face types.

Special Exhaust

Special exhaust systems are required when a retail store has a working kitchen or otherwise produces strong odors or fumes. In a multistory building, the landlord will provide a special exhaust duct, to which the tenant can connect to remove contaminated air from the kitchen, bathroom, or other space. This air will not be recirculated through the HVAC system, but will be channeled outside. If the retail store is directly below a roof, special exhaust can be ducted outside through the roof.

Controls

Temperature controls in retail stores are either electric or pneumatic. Both thermostat types sense air temperature and turn the system on or off in response to temperature changes. Electric thermostats are either line voltage (over 30 volts) or low voltage. Typically, space temperature electric controls are low voltage. Pneumatic controls operate by air pressure instead of electricity. Pressurized control air is provided by the landlord and supplied to the retail store in a small, capped, copper tube.

Insulation

Supply-air ductwork may be isolated from the fan unit by a flexible connection and lined with accoustical board to reduce the transmission of noise from the air-handling unit to the space. This may be required only for the first ten feet, or may be installed throughout the system. Supply ductwork is also installed with insulation wrapped on its exterior to help maintain the temperature of the conditioned air.

ELECTRICAL SYSTEMS

Electrical systems supply electricity for outlets, lighting (as discussed in chapter 6), equipment, and sometimes heating. In larger shopping malls, tenants will usually be required to complete the entire electrical installation within their space, while in smaller strip centers all basic electricity and lighting may be provided by the landlord (fig. 7-14).

Service Equipment

The electrical system of a shopping center is designed to satisfy average electrical use. The landlord will, therefore, stipulate the maximum electrical load the tenant may place on the building's system. An industry standard for this service is 15 watts per square foot of area. In a shopping mall, power distribution points are usually located in service corridors at the rear of stores. The merchant may have to run an electrical feeder to this point of connection, or, as happens frequently, the landlord extends an empty conduit from a distribution point to within the store and the merchant completes the necessary wiring. Power may

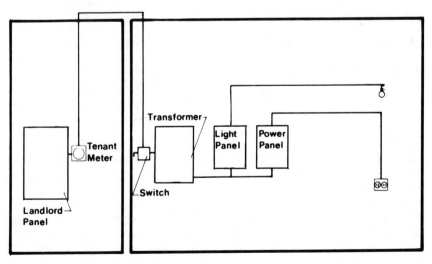

Tenant Space

7-14. Line diagram of a typical electrical system for a retail store located in a shopping center.

be made available to the tenant at 120 volts or higher, such as 277V, which the tenant must then transform. Larger stores may use 277 volts of power for fluorescent lighting with considerable savings in material costs, since the size of conductors (wire) can be smaller when higher voltage is used. If required, a transformer to convert higher-voltage power to 120V should be installed in a tenant service area, and may be either floor-mounted or suspended on a platform if space considerations dictate. Since transformers can weigh hundreds of pounds, care should be taken in detailing its support structure. Under most codes, a service switch (main power disconnect) must be provided before the panel within five feet of entry into the building.

Panelboards receive and distribute transformed power and the circuit breakers it contains disconnect power if overuse of power occurs. Panelboards are usually located in a back room and should be convenient to store employees and easily accessible, if used for store switching or in case of circuit overload. The panelboard cabinet can be either flush mounted in the wall or surface mounted. Surface-mounted panels are placed on a plywood backboard and mounted to the wall; the backboard should be large enough to accommodate all other wall-mounted electrical and telephone equipment as well. Lighting and power circuits may be combined on one panel, but good practice dictates a separate panel for each. For smaller electrical loading conditions, a split-bus panel that separates lighting and power circuits within a single panel may be used.

Distribution

Electrical power is distributed from the panelboard to outlets, fixtures, and other devices via insulated copper conductors usually enclosed in metal conduit (pipe). Some jurisdictions permit the use of BX or other armored cables instead of conduits, which results in a less expensive but less flexible installation. If flexibility for future electrical changes is desirable, conduit should be a minimum of ¾ inch in diameter. Since the ceilings of many retail stores are fully accessible, additional conduit runs or rewiring can be accomplished without interrupting store business. If the space above the ceiling is used as a return air plenum, the electrical equipment and connections above the ceiling will have to conform to the code requirements for use in plenum ceilings. These special electrical and lighting fixtures and connections are more expensive and must be specifically designated.

Store Fixtures

When installing conduit and wiring for lighting or power in store fixtures such as cash counters, the service may be "roughed-in" to a junction box near the store fixture; a short section of flexible conduit and wiring known as a "whip" is then used to make the final connection. When this method is used, the store fixtures can be moved around somewhat for access, adjustment, or cleaning. Electrical power for store fixtures can be routed through the ceiling, wall, or floor. However, routing conduits through the floor is more expensive and difficult because the floor must be channeled or cored, which also may involve working in another tenant's space. In some areas, local codes allow store fixtures to be prewired, which can result in substantial savings of time and money. However, other jurisdictions require all wiring to be done on-site. Local restrictions must be verified before construction is begun.

Receptacles and Switches

The number and location of duplex power outlets is not usually specified by code for retail spaces, although codes may require receptacles in show windows. However, designers must plan for an appropriate number of receptacles for cleaning equipment, cash registers, office equipment, movable lamps and displays, and other equipment required by the store. Certain cash registers or computers may require a dedicated (individual, separate) circuit or an isolated (individual, separate, in its own conduit) circuit. Designers may wish to use decorator-type receptacles and switches for those that are visible to the public. These are available in many colors and are contemporary in design (figs. 7-15, 7-16).

Typically, all switching for lighting and power—either the panelboard circuit breakers or a contactor switch that acts as a relay to switch a series of circuits simultaneously—is located in back-room areas.

7-15. *Left:* **A decorator electrical outlet.** *(Courtesy of Slater Electric, Inc.)*

7-16. *Right:* **Contemporary electrical switch.** *(Courtesy of Slater Electric, Inc.)*

Communication Systems

The retail store may install a sound system to provide internal paging, emergency paging, and/or background music. Speakers for paging may be spaced at about twice the distance of a sound system designed for high quality music; that is, a 12-foot spacing for paging only, and a 6-foot spacing for quality music rendition. Of course, the entire sound system is upgraded from amplifiers to speakers to increase the sound quality for proper music reproduction. Because music is usually provided from a recorded source (cassette tapes or records), the tenant who airs recorded music for the public should be aware that he must pay royalty fees. (The tenant should consult the local musicians' union for more information.) Most jurisdictions permit low-voltage wiring, such as that for sound and telephone systems, to be run loose (not in conduit) in a plenum ceiling. If speakers are required for building emergency paging, these will be connected to the building system. When necessary, emergency announcements will be made on all the speakers in the system, thus overriding any music playing in the store.

Emergency Lighting

Most jurisdictions will require some form of store emergency lighting that is activated in a power failure and provides the minimum illumination necessary for shoppers to exit the store safely. Because most shopping malls do not provide a source of emergency power, battery operated units must be used. Many different self-contained units, which contain self-charging batteries to power the emergency light, are available. The battery container may be located in a service area while the light fixture can be exposed to public view. These fixtures may be located on a wall at the ceiling line or in the ceiling. Some battery-powered emergency lights have an appearance similar to a typical fluorescent troffer.

Illuminated exit signs indicating the location of an approved fire exit should be installed above each exit. These signs may also contain a recharging battery to light the sign in the event of a power failure. An attractive exit sign, from a design standpoint, is a sheet of clear Plexiglas with the ballast and battery concealed in the wall or ceiling.

SECURITY SYSTEMS

In shopping malls, security systems are usually installed only in high-risk stores, such as jewelry and fur shops. Malls usually have effective security personnel on twenty-four-hour patrol, and the entire complex is locked after hours. In-line stores, either in strip centers or on the street, may require security systems for retail use. It is advisable to use physical security devices, such as bars and grilles, in addition to an electrical alarm to increase store security in the event of power cutoff or if response to an alarm is delayed. When the retail store is open for business, most alarm systems are down and the merchant's concern is to control shoplifting or possibly robbery. After hours, the storeowner's concern is to prevent burglary, arson, and vandalism. Security systems are available through special consultants or central station operators.

Shoplifting and Robbery Control

Closed-circuit television cameras can be installed to monitor areas of the store not visible to store personnel from the cash counter. The counter, if located toward the front of the store, provides a line of defense against shoplifters; extended visibility will be available to personnel if monitors are located in the counter. If the cash counter is within the camera's view, monitors will usually be located elsewhere, such as in an office, in an effort to control robbery. The presence of the visible cameras is intimidating to some thieves. Ceiling convex mirrors perform the same function and permit sales help to view a greater portion of the store from a single location.

Entry-sensing devices are useful when a salesperson is serving a customer and his attention is focused on making the sale. Shoplifters frequently work as teams, with one engaging the salesperson's attention while the other steals the goods. Anyone entering the store can be announced by the sound of a tone, bell, buzzer, clicker, or light, if the door is monitored with a motion detector. Entry-sensing detectors can also be microwave, ultrasonic, infrared, photo cell, door-hinge contactor, or a hidden floor mat.

Exit alarms are activated by merchandise tagged with special devices to sound an alarm if these special tags are removed from the store. Because the tags are difficult to remove without special tools, they are an effective shoplifting deterrent. Exit doors can be alarmed locally and activated when opened. Local contactor alarms can also be placed on safes or in other high-security areas. Often a mandatory second exit for a store is available only through a storeroom, which will necessitate leaving the storeroom door unlocked. It may be prudent, where possible, to keep the storeroom locked and to locate the exit elsewhere. An employee-operated panic alarm can be placed at the cash counter or elsewhere to sound a local audible alarm or signal a central station in the event of a robbery or other emergency.

Burglary, Arson, and Vandalism Control

Entry sensors such as those that protect against shoplifting can also be installed to defend against after-hour intruders. These will not sound an audible alarm, but will signal the central station monitor. The central station is a privately operated, off-premises company that maintains twenty-four-hour personnel to monitor signal panels. The entry-sensor signal light is activated automatically when an intruder enters the store. The signal from the sensor is sent to an automatic telephone dialer, and the alarm is transmitted over regular telephone lines. Central system personnel will then dispatch their own security person or notify the police of the break-in. Systems that direct their alarm to the police are generally not used, however, because of the high incidence of false alarms. Other similar sensing devices may be located throughout the store to detect intruders entering through walls, floors, or ceilings.

GLOSSARY

Aluminum storefront sections Aluminum that has been extruded to form hollow, rectangular sections used as mullions and muntins in storefront construction.

Bay window Window(s) projecting outward from a wall.

Biparting door A double door whose two leaves slide away from each other in the same plane and meet at the center line of the door.

Coffer A deeply recessed ceiling panel.

Corner store A store located at the outside corner intersection of two malls or streets.

Demising wall A wall that separates one tenant from another or one tenant from a common area, such as a service corridor, in a shopping center.

Direct glare Glare resulting from inadequately shielded light sources in the field of view.

Electrical ballasts In discharge-type light fixtures, ballast supplies the high voltage to start the arc and then limits the current in the arc.

Emergency egress The path leading to a fire exit or fire-protected exit corridor.

Enclosed mall A shopping center building having a centrally heated and air-conditioned enclosed public circulation space that serves to connect all the stores.

Fascia A horizontal band above the storefront doors and windows, upon which a store sign is often placed.

Flame spread rating A numerical designation (from 0 to 100) indicating the resistance of a building material to flaming combustion over its surface. A noncombustible material has a rating of 0.

Footcandle The unit used to measure the amount of light that reaches a surface. Footcandles equal lumens divided by the area illuminated in square feet.

Footlambert A unit of brightness equal to the emission from a light source or surface reflection of one lumen per square foot of area illuminated.

Freestanding store A shop or department store located on a site attached to no other building, which may have adjacent parking on all sides.

Furring strips Continuous metal channels that are attached parallel to walls at regularly spaced intervals and to which drywall is screwed in wall construction.

Glazing Installing glass in windows, doors, or storefronts.

Gold leaf Very thin sheets of rolled gold used in gilding or inscribing glass, as for signs.

Gross leasable area (GLA) The total leasable area of a store. Usually, this is the actual store area between the demising walls and the lease line at the storefront.

Gypsum board A wallboard with a paper finish and a core of gypsum plaster.

In-line store A store located between two other stores in a shopping center or on a street.

Lowest qualified bid The lowest price to complete the proposed construction submitted by a bidder deemed qualified to perform the work satisfactorily.

Lumen A unit of luminous flux or quantity of light.

Mullions Vertical members separating and supporting windows, doors, or panels set in a series.

Muntins Horizontal members that separate and support windows, doors, or panels.

National tenant A merchant who operates a chain of stores.

Noise reduction coefficient (NRC) The average amount of sound energy absorbed by a material over a range of frequencies between 250 Hz and 2,000 Hz.

Open mall A shopping center composed of separate buildings arranged to form a central outdoor circulation space connecting all the stores.

Photometric brightness The amount of footlamberts emitted or reflected from a light source or surface.

Pin mounting A method of sign attachment in which the sign letters are pinned to the sign background.

Plenum The space between a ceiling and the floor or roof above, sometimes used as an air duct.

Program A written compilation of all project functions, their relationships, and their space requirements.

Rail A horizontal piece in a door or window.

Sales volume The gross dollar amount of retail sales for a store in a given period, usually expressed as a factor of total store area.

Silicone A sealant used to hold glass in a frame or to seal the joint between two glass panels.

Smoke density factor A numerical designation (from 0 to 100) of a building material indicating its surface burning characteristics and how much smoke it produces. A noncombustible material has a rating of 0.

Soffit The exposed undersurface of any overhead component of a building, such as an arch, beam, or cornice.

Sound batting Insulation installed in a wall to absorb sound.

Sound reverberation The persistent echoing of previously generated sound, caused by the reflection of acoustic waves from the surfaces of enclosed spaces.

Specifications A part of the contract documents. Specifications are in written form and detail the items of construction to be purchased and methods of installation.

Spectral distribution The separation of the component colors of light plotted to indicate the relative amounts of wavelength energy.

Sprinkler test drain A point in the fire-protection sprinkler line that permits local drainage of the piping after pressure testing.

Strip center A shopping center with buildings sited to permit parking directly adjacent to shops and views of individual shops from adjacent roadways.

Stub-in A utility duct (such as water, sewer, sprinkler, or electric) connecting a main source to a point within the tenant's premises.

UL rating Underwriters Laboratories (UL) is an independent organization that tests materials and equipment for fire and shock hazards and establishes and maintains standards. UL reviews and tests building components and provides a fire-resistance rating, stated in hours of fire resistance.

BIBLIOGRAPHY

Architectural Aluminum Manufacturers Association. 1977. *Aluminum storefront and entrance design guide manual.* Chicago: Architectural Aluminum Manufacturers Association.

The Architectural Woodwork Institute. 1984. *Architectural woodwork.* Arlington, VA: Architectural Woodwork Institute.

The Carpet and Rug Institute. 1980. *Carpet specifier's handbook.* Dalton, GA: Carpet and Rug Institute.

Cialdini, Robert B. 1984. *Influence: How and why people agree on things.* New York: William Morrow & Co.

Denby, Carol, ed. 1986. *The best of store design.* Locust Valley, NY: PCB International.

Evans, Bill. 1981. *Shopfronts.* New York: Van Nostrand Reinhold Co.

Eysenck, Hans J., and Michael Eysenck. 1983. *Mindwatching: Why people behave the way they do.* New York: Doubleday/Anchor Press.

Hopkins, Tom. 1982. *How to master the art of selling.* New York: Warner Books.

Illuminating Engineering Society of North America. 1976. Lighting merchandising areas. New York: Illuminating Engineering Society. Pamphlet.

Mang, Karl. 1982. *New shops.* New York: Architectural Book Publishing Co.

McGuiness, William J., Benjamin Stein, and John S. Reynolds. 1980. *Mechanical and electrical equipment for buildings.* New York: John Wiley & Sons.

National Fire Protection Association. 1983. *Installation of sprinkler systems: NFPA 13.* Quincy, MA: National Fire Protection Association. Pamphlet.

Novak, Adolph. 1977. *Store planning and design.* New York: Lebhar-Friedman Books.

Nuckolls, James L. 1983. *Interior lighting for environmental designers.* New York: John Wiley & Sons.

Peglar, Martin M. 1982. *The language of store planning and display.* New York: Fairchild Publications.

Peglar, Martin M., ed. 1984. *Stores of the year.* Vol. III. New York: Retail Reporting Corp.

Russell, Beverly, ed. 1981. *The Interiors book of shops and restaurants.* New York: Watson-Guptill.

Slater, Walter L. 1974. *Floors and floor maintenance.* New York: John Wiley & Sons.

Tile Council of America, Inc. 1981. *American national standard specifications for ceramic tile.* Princeton, NJ: Tile Council of America, Inc.

Weismantel, Guy E. 1981. *Paint handbook.* New York: McGraw-Hill.

Wood Products Association. 1985. *The wood book.* Seattle: Commerce Publishing Corp.

APPENDIX

CHECKLIST OF PROGRAM ITEMS FOR RETAIL STORE DESIGN

Store Name _____

Location _____

Size _____

A. General

1. What is the store's construction budget?
2. What is the schedule for store opening?
3. Have the base drawings and lease documents from the landlord been received?
4. Has a builder been selected?
5. Who will represent the storeowner in making design decisions?

B. Image

1. How will your customers be drawn to the store?
   a. They will be directed to the store by advertising or other promotion.
   b. They will be attracted to the store as they pass by.
2. How will customers select products?
   a. Most products will be displayed openly. Adequate product-evaluation information will be located at the sales point.

b. Most products will be in closed displays and sales personnel will be available to provide product-evaluation information.
3. What is the image of the store?
a. Exclusive or popular
b. Traditional or avant-garde
c. Popularly priced or expensive
d. Serious or playful
e. Service oriented or self-service
f. Quiet or noisy
g. Subdued or spirited
h. Cool or warm
i. Smooth or rough
4. What is the market for the store's products?
a. Young, middle-aged, older
b. Men, women, boys, girls
c. Below-average, average, or above-average income level
5. Are there any other stores that you find attractive and relevant to the design of this store?

C. Spatial Organization
1. How will the circulation paths be designed?
a. On one level or multilevels?
b. Can a shopper evaluate products from a circulation area or is the circulation space solely to permit movement from one area to another?
2. What is the best location for the cash counter?
a. In the front, middle, or rear of the store?
3. Can products be displayed in or on the cash counter?
4. Will the wrapping counter be separate from the cash counter?
5. What percentage of the store should be devoted to storage? Which items will be stored?
6. Is a public washroom desirable? Are separate employee washrooms desirable? (Check local codes)
7. Should employee kitchen, dining, or locker facilities be provided?
8. Is special equipment required for repair or production? If so, what are its spatial and mechanical/electrical requirements?
9. How many employees will work in the store at any one time? What will their roles be?
10. How and where will sales be transacted?
11. How and where will money be stored?
12. Will the store deliver products?
13. How will store deliveries be made?
14. Will any offices be required?

D. Product Display
1. Which items will be displayed?
   a. By group, such as men's suits, men's shoes, women's shoes.
   b. By type of purchase, such as staples, convenience, and impulse items.
2. What percentage of total display area will each product require?
3. What are the qualities of each product to be displayed?
   a. Size: large/small
   b. Class: unique/common
   c. Price: expensive/inexpensive
4. What display techniques shall be used for each product?
   a. Presentation: massed/individual
   b. Support: from above/from below
   c. Integration: isolated/contextual
5. Which products will require special displays or display techniques?
6. How will the customer evaluate each product?
   a. Review its surface qualities—color, texture, and so on.
   b. Review its shape or outline.
   c. Salesperson will be present to assist in the evaluation.
   d. Written product-evaluation material will be present at the display.

E. Storefronts (verify landlord requirements)
1. How will the storefront be designed?
   a. Transparency: open/closed
   b. Plan: recessed/projected
   c. Design statement: strong/neutral
2. Will specific products be displayed in show windows or will the entire store be visible through the storefront show windows?
3. If show windows will be used to display merchandise, will the show windows be backed or unbacked?
4. Will the customer be required to open a door to enter the store or will he or she simply pass through an opening?
5. Has a store logo been developed as the basis for a store sign?

F. Materials
1. What are the preferred materials for the store?
   a. Walls
   b. Floors
   c. Ceilings
   d. Storefront
   e. Fixtures and furniture

G. Systems

1. Is there a preference for a specific lighting source?
    a. Incandescent
    b. Fluorescent
    c. Metal halide
2. Are any types of light fixtures undesirable?
    a. Recessed cans
    b. Exposed lighting, such as neon, cold cathode, or incandescent
    c. Track lights
    d. Surface-mounted fixtures
    e. Ambient up-lighting
3. What are the security requirements for merchandise, money, and employees?
    a. Cameras
    b. Monitoring devices
    c. Panic buttons
    d. Safes or strongboxes
    e. Security patrol
4. Are there special requirements for cooling or heating any areas of the store?
5. Are any products, people, or equipment susceptible to damage from excess heat, cold, moisture, dryness, light, noise, or air flow?
6. Will there be a sound system in the store?
7. Where will telephones be required?
8. Where will electrical outlets be required?
    a. Are special isolated or dedicated outlets required for computer equipment or cash registers?
9. Is a water source required for any location?

INDEX